M

The
Mummy Market

The
Mummy Market

by
Nancy Brelis

Pictures by
Ben Shecter

Harper & Row, Publishers • New York, Evanston, and London

For Doron,
  Janie,
   Tia,
    and Matthew

Contents

And through the glass window shines the sun.
How should I love, and I so young?
   The bailey beareth the bell away;
   The lily, the lily, the rose I lay.

—Unknown

CHAPTER 1

The Martins' Doom

Elizabeth Martin was late home from school. She had been asked to stay after class and write, "I will not pass notes during arithmetic" a hundred times. She was pedaling at top speed, head down and braids streaming out behind her. When she turned the corner into Ash Street, she leaned back and coasted no-hands up to her house. She glanced at the closed front door, and looked away toward the backyard. She saw that the red flag, signaling an Important Meeting, was hanging from the tree house, so she left her bike where it was, and ran to the foot of the big maple tree.

"The Rose and The Sword Forever," she said, and the rope ladder was tossed down. A small face with messy brown hair appeared at the edge of the platform.

"Boy, we thought you were never coming," said her sister Jenny, who was ten.

"When you're in the sixth grade, just pray you don't get Miss Hunter," said Elizabeth. "Boy, what an eagle eye!"

"Did you get sent to The Office?" said Harry anxiously. He was six.

"No. Just had to write 'I will not pass notes during arithmetic' a hundred times."

"You poor kid," said Jenny.

"It isn't too bad if you do it down instead of sideways, and write 'I, I, I, I, will, will, will,' like that," said Elizabeth.

She climbed the rope ladder (which is harder than it looks), and pulled it up after her.

The children sometimes felt that the tree house was more their home than the old brown house they lived in with their housekeeper. Her real name was Mrs. Hinchley, but the children called her The Gloom.

It had taken them all the summer before to build the tree house, and the money from allowances and lemonade stands and from catching

old Mrs. Cavour's rose bugs at one cent for ten bugs had all gone to the lumberyard, or Samson's Hardware Store. But it had been worth all of it. If instead of parents you have a very responsible housekeeper who puts duty first and children second, you need an escape. Tree houses are perfect for privacy of all kinds: Important Meetings, and plain peace and quiet.

Mrs. Hinchley was tall, pale, and efficient. She smelled of Clorox, and never forgot to remind the children to brush their teeth. Once, for a few days, Jenny had avoided a daily bath by washing her knees and mussing up the towel, but this was soon discovered and no one dared try it again. The girls' dresses were always perfectly starched and ironed, but if Harry had a bad dream he got into Elizabeth's bed, not Mrs. Hinchley's. If Jenny was unhappy because a friend at school had been unkind, she told Elizabeth about it, not Mrs. Hinchley. Elizabeth, who was nearly twelve, had no one to talk to about the unrest she sometimes felt but couldn't put into words, even to Jenny, because she hardly knew herself what the matter was. Some things, practical things, like what happens if you touch a deadly nightshade berry and then lick your finger, she could ask their friend Mrs. Cavour. (The answer is: nothing at all.)

Mrs. Cavour was so old and brown and wrinkled that it seemed possible that she had always been there, like a mountain or a river. She knew all about every plant and flower that grows. She was little and bright-eyed, and sometimes when she squatted, studying a wilted flower, she looked like a chipmunk. She smelled of acorns, or the earth in a thick forest. She lived on the edge of the suburb the children's house was in, and she had lived there when it had all been farms and woods. Even though houses had grown up around hers, she still seemed to be a country person. Elizabeth had met her on her first explorings beyond their own neighborhood, when her first two-wheeler was new.

Now Elizabeth bunched up the rope ladder on the edge of the platform, and turning to her sister, said, "What's the meeting about?"

"We've got to do something," said Jenny. "The Gloom flushed Harry's tadpoles down the toilet."

"I raised them from eggs," said Harry in a choking voice.

"Even The Rotten Eyeball?" said Elizabeth. The Rotten Eyeball was Harry's biggest tadpole, and was so named because of his white belly and his huge size.

Harry nodded silently, and tears came to his eyes.

"Boy! Grinchley Hinchley," said Elizabeth.

"We can't stand it anymore," said Jenny. "I wish *she* would get flushed down the toilet."

Elizabeth was frightened. "Take it back," she said. "Take it back."

"Oh, all right," said Jenny. "I take it back, I take it back, a hundred thousand times."

Elizabeth felt mean.

"Harry," she said, "you flushed my turtle down the toilet."

"Elizabeth!" said Jenny.

"Well, you called me Harrington, and I thought that's what you did to turtles. I was only three," said Harry.

"I flushed your turtle down because he was dead. You just came and took mine when I was at school."

"Stop it," shouted Jenny. "You're ruining our meeting."

"I'm sorry," said Elizabeth. "I didn't mean it, Harry."

"That's all right," said Harry. "What are we going to do about The Gloom?"

"The Martin's doom
Is to live with The Gloom.
Boom, Boom, Boom," said Jenny.

"Boom, Boom, Boom," said Harry.

"If we make so much noise, she'll hear us," said Elizabeth. "Hey, I've got an idea. Jenny, you sneak into the house and pinch the telephone book."

"What for?" said Jenny.

"I'll tell you when we get it."

"Go get it yourself then, bossy."

"Oh, all right," said Elizabeth, who didn't want to start another fight.

She climbed down the ladder and ran across the yard. She opened the back door quietly, and hearing the vacuum cleaner going in the living room, she tiptoed across the kitchen to the telephone, picked up the book, and tiptoed out unseen.

Back in the tree house she turned the pages eagerly, then searched one page and looked up. "It's no good," she said. "It's not here. They have one for animals, but not for children."

"What?" said Jenny.

"The Society for Prevention of Cruelty to

7

Children," said Elizabeth. "I read about it in a book. But they don't have one. The book didn't tell the truth."

"Let's run away," said Jenny. "We can go out in the world to seek our fortunes."

"Can I bring my tractor and my road-grader and my iguana?" said Harry.

"Sure, and I'll bring my recorder and my bear," said Jenny.

"We haven't any place to run to. They'd find us. We'd have to take the wheelbarrow, anyway, to carry all those things," said Elizabeth.

"We could go on that television show, Kiddie's Questions, and win some money and take a train to The West," said Jenny.

"You know what we'd win, I bet?" said Elizabeth. "An electric organ and free lessons for one whole year, plus bonus gift of a game of Parchesi for each little kiddie in the family."

"Well, what can we do then?" said Jenny.

"Let's go see Mrs. Cavour," said Harry. "She might be able to make The Gloom go up in smoke."

"She can't do real magic, silly," said Elizabeth. "She's just old and funny and always saying poetry. It isn't real spells."

"How do you know?" said Jenny. "She talks to her flowers and they grow better than anyone else's, don't they? Anyway, she listens to you when you talk to her, which is more than most grown-ups do."

"She never says, 'Yes, dear,' when you ask her how far it is to the moon or something," said Harry.

"Okay. We better see if she has any ideas," said Elizabeth. "But I bet they'll be too screwy to try."

"*E-li*-zabeth, *Ha*-rrington, *Jen*-nifer, come in at once. Where are you?"

It was The Gloom calling.

They climbed down from the tree house and ran across to the back door. The Gloom was standing there waving a sponge around as she talked.

"Elizabeth, you haven't started your homework, and you must set the table tonight in half an hour. Now, quickly, get up to your room.

"Jennifer, your closet is disgraceful. No wonder you run out of socks, if you just throw them in there with the books and toys. Go to your room at once, and don't come down till that closet is immaculate.

"Harrington! Look at your trucks all over

9

the yard. What will the neighbors think? Pick them up at once and put them in the cellar."

"Yes, Mrs. Hinchley," said the children, as if repeating an old sad chant.

"Why you can't learn to do the things you are obliged to do in an orderly and consistent manner, I do not know," said The Gloom.

"Yes, Mrs. Hinchley," said the children. If they had listened to her, they might have realized that they didn't understand what she meant; but they had long ago learned to close their ears and say, "Yes, Mrs. Hinchley," at proper intervals.

"Can I go pick up my trucks now?" said Harry.

"*May* I, Harrington!" said The Gloom. "Yes, you may."

The children fled to their separate tasks, each thinking that tomorrow was Saturday and surely they would be able to sneak off to Mrs. Cavour's house.

CHAPTER 2

Mrs. Cavour's Garden

Mrs. Cavour's garden and house were surrounded by a huge and impenetrable hedge. It
was made of eglantine, sweetbrier, musk rose,
and other dense, thorny, but lovely and fragrant,
bushes; and twined throughout were other dis-
couragements to intruders, like poison ivy and
deadly nightshade vines. In no place could you
see through the hedge, it was so thick and old.
Hundreds of birds nested in its safety—catbirds,
brown thrashers, song sparrows, yellow throats,
and robins.

There was only one gate in the hedge, and
through this—startling the birds into hurried

flights—the children wheeled their bikes. It was almost a tunnel, darkened by the branches meeting overhead and silent except for the bees. You could hear Mrs. Cavour's hedge before you came near it when it was blooming. It was early June and too early for the eglantine, but the sweetbrier was in bloom and the hedge was truly a "bee-loud glade."

The children were silent, always somewhat in awe as they entered the garden. Not a silence as if there were a rule bidding them keep quiet, but rather a feeling that in a little while they would run and leap and shout; just now they would be still and feel how the garden was. So much life in one place, so much order and disorder, peace and activity, color and cool green: poppies that seemed to be straining to be a more burning red; and white and blue iris, stiff and patient; cool shade and hurried, urgent hummingbirds and careless butterflies. The garden was a wild and marvelous mixture—pale lettuce was growing with the fragile and airy columbine. Tomato vines were crawling up stakes half-hidden by peonies looking heavy and lazy with their full pink and white blooms. Climbing roses and cucumber and gourd vines, clematis

vines, beanstalks and grapevines crawled over
trellises and covered the small house almost
completely. Foxgloves, lupines, lemon lilies,
sweet william, valerian, painted daisy, feverfew,
and pinks were blossoming mixed in with spin-
ach, carrots, beets, dill, and parsley. In one
corner hollyhocks and hills of corn were begin-
ning to push up their stalks. New smells, as one
walked stepping on thyme or passing the basil or

lemon verbena in the warm sun, were mixed in the air. Bluets, wood violets, and wild strawberries grew in the lawn, and in the shade were lady slippers, trillium, and star flowers, pipsissewa, and rattlesnake plantain.

"There she is," said Harry, "over by that white bush."

They ran across the grass and found her cutting asparagus and putting it in a basket.

"Hullo, Mrs. Cavour," said Jenny. "Why does your asparagus grow all by itself with nothing mixed in?"

"Well, Jenny," said Mrs. Cavour, "asparagus is different from other plants. You put salt on it to kill the weeds, and it kills everything but the asparagus."

Mrs. Cavour stood up and shook her basket to settle the asparagus in it. "Once there was a Roman emperor who used to say '*Celerius quam asparagi cocuntur*,' " she said. "That means 'As quick as you can cook asparagus.' He was a very unusual man."

"Did you know him?" said Harry.

"Not personally," said Mrs. Cavour, "but some of my relatives were acquainted with him."

"Mrs. Cavour, we have a terrible problem," said Elizabeth.

"We have to do something about The Gloom," said Harry.

"I wondered when you would come to that conclusion," said Mrs. Cavour.

"What shall we do?" said Jenny. "We can't stand her any longer."

"I believe I can help you," said Mrs. Cavour. "There is one very possible solution."

"What's a possible solution?" asked Harry. "Will it make her go up in smoke?"

"Oh, Harry," said Elizabeth.

"That is quite out of fashion," said Mrs. Cavour. "Nowadays we try to get the same effect by more subtle means. However, if you will bear with me, I must keep up my professional appearances. Jenny, will you get some of those yellow lilies under the lilac bush there, and, Elizabeth, run and find some white columbine. Harry, take this knife and cut a spray of sweetbriar from the hedge. Don't run with the knife. I'll be right back."

"Oh, Jenny," whispered Elizabeth, when she had gone, "she's just going to have some nutty flower magic. It isn't real, and it isn't going to help about The Gloom."

"Well, it's fun, anyway," said Jenny. "Let's see what she does."

15

Mrs. Cavour and Harry returned, Mrs. Cavour carrying a mixed bunch of flowers and leaves.

"Now, children," she said, "sit down and say the names of these flowers with me, and repeat them with me when we come to them in the magic: Lily, germander, and sops in wine." She held them up one by one as she named them. "Sweetbrier, bonfire, strawberry wire, and columbine. Now, here we go. Pay attention, and come in with the chorus."

She gathered all the flowers together, and seemed to be gathering herself in concentration. Then with a merry smile, as if at a joke, she began:

Can the physician make sick men well?
Can the magician a fortune divine?
Without
　　Lily, germander, and sops in wine,
　　　　with sweetbrier
　　　　and bonfire
　　　　and strawberry wire
　　　　and columbine.
Within and without, in and out, round as a ball,
With hither and thither, as straight as a line
With
　　Lily, germander, and sops in wine,
　　　　with sweetbrier
　　　　and bonfire
　　　　and strawberry wire
　　　　and columbine.
When Saturn did live, there lived no poor,
The King and the beggar with roots did dine
With
　　Lily, germander, and sops in wine,
　　　　with sweetbrier
　　　　and bonfire
　　　　and strawberry wire
　　　　and columbine.

"Thank you, children. You were a great help. Now let me tell you what I suggest. You must go to the Mummy Market."

"The what?" said Jenny and Elizabeth. Harry was sitting still with his mouth and his eyes wide open.

"The Mummy Market, my dears. It is many years since I have been there, and it may not be still in operation. Anyhow, it is worth a try."

"Mrs. Cavour, are you teasing us?" said Elizabeth.

"Have I ever teased you, my dear? Your position is a serious one indeed."

"Where's the Mummy Market?" asked Harry.

"Well, it used to be just beyond Central Square, and I can't imagine that it has moved. Of course, it is only open for business on Thursdays from three to five. Take the bus to Revere Square and get a transfer for the subway. Catch an express car for Central Square, and when you come up, turn to the right towards the old Center Church. Go down Guernsey Street till you come to the open market—where the people with stalls are selling vegetables and flowers. Notice the clock tower at the head of the market place, and just to the right of it should be a small alley—Childer's Lane, it was called. Follow that to its end, and there you will find the Mummy Market—if you find it at all."

"What's a Mummy Market, Mrs. Cavour?" asked Jenny.

"You'll see when you get there, my dear, and now you must run along. June is a very busy month for me, and although I have enjoyed your visit, I must get back to my work. Come and see me again when you have been to the Mummy Market, and let me know what success you have had."

"Thank you, Mrs. Cavour," said Elizabeth.

"Good-bye, Mrs. Cavour. Good-bye," said Jenny and Harry.

Back in the tree house Mrs. Cavour's suggestion seemed even more impossible than it had in her strange and fragrant garden.

"I told you she'd have some nutty ideas," said Elizabeth.

"It's not nutty. Mrs. Cavour isn't nutty. You're nutty, nutty, nutty," said Harry.

"Well, you think what you like," said Jenny. "Harry and I are going next Thursday. You can come if you want to."

"Oh, Elizabeth, please come," wailed Harry. "I don't want to go on the subway without you. Suppose we get lost? Please don't be that way."

Elizabeth put her arms around Harry. "Of course, I'll come, and even if there isn't any Mummy Market, we'll have an expedition next Thursday for sure," she said.

CHAPTER 3

The Mummy Market

The bell in the clock tower was striking three o'clock as the three children came into the vegetable market on Thursday afternoon.

"Fresh native lettuce, two heads for a quarter," called a man as they passed.

"Hey, girlie, take your mother a bunch of flowers, only two bits," called another.

"Get your strawberries here, none better in the city. Thirty-nine cents a box," called a fat lady with a white apron.

"Tomatoes, red tomatoes, vine-ripened," called a man whose cart was full of squashy-looking tomatoes.

"They'd be good to throw at someone," whispered Jenny.

On they walked till they stood at the foot of the clock tower. Next to it stood a line of stores with open fronts, selling meat, poultry, and fish.

WE SPECIALIZE IN SAUSAGES
HOT, SWEET, POLISH, ITALIAN, PORTUGUESE
YOU NAME IT — WE'VE GOT IT

said a large sign.

Between the stores and the tower was only a dark alley, some of its cobblestones patched with lumps of asphalt. A small blue-and-white sign on the wall of the first store said:

CHILDER'S LANE

"Look," said Jenny. "It's there."

"Boy! It's real," said Harry. "Let's go."

"It goes around a corner; I can't see anyone down there," said Elizabeth doubtfully.

"Oh, come *on*," said Jenny, starting ahead down the alley.

The brick walls on either side towered up and shut out the sounds from the market as well as the sunlight. They walked single file cautiously. Jenny first, then Harry, and then Elizabeth. The alley turned to the left around the back of the tower, and as they rounded the corner they could see that it ended in a small open square. They stopped, still in the shadow of the alley, and looked with growing excitement at the activity going on before them.

The two long sides of the narrow square were lined with large stalls—like booths at a fair (where you get three darts for a dime), only bigger, and obviously from their solid look, permanently in place. They looked like many small stages, and each had one woman in it, like a single actress. All the women were doing different things, and on each stage the scenery was different. The cobbled center of the square was full of children, boys and girls of all ages, talking to each other and to the ladies in the booths. A steady hum of conversation could be heard mixed with confused music. One of the ladies was sitting cross-legged, singing with a guitar, and another was playing something quite different on a piano.

In the center was a tiny building with windows on all sides. It had a sign saying:

MUMMY MARKET INFORMATION BOOTH

Against the far wall of the square was a bicycle rack and some old hitching posts, to one of which a howling puppy was tied. There was a big sign over the bicycle rack that said:

THIS MUMMY MARKET
IS RUN BY CHILDREN FOR CHILDREN
PLEASE OBSERVE ALL THE REGULATIONS

Posters were stuck irregularly on the wall near the big sign.

WHY PUT UP WITH AN
UNSATISFACTORY MOTHER?
COME TO THE
MUMMY MARKET
AND FIND THE RIGHT ONE FOR YOU

said one poster.

CHANGE YOUR MOTHER
FOR ANOTHER!
ONE THAT'S NEW
IS FUN FOR YOU!

said one below it.

"Gee whiz," whispered Jenny.

"Let's go in," said Harry.

Still only half believing it, they walked into the sunlight from the alley, and turned toward the nearest stall.

It was decorated like a warm and homelike kitchen. In it a plump lady with bright red hair, wearing an apron covered with pink dots, was making cookies. She was handing them out to the crowd of children standing in front. "Can you make chocolate cake too?" asked a little boy, munching on a cookie.

"Of course I can, honey," said the lady.

"With thick frosting?" asked Harry.

"Naturally, sweetie-pie," said the smiling lady.

"Do you get mad if children just pick off the frosting and leave the cake?" said a skinny girl with thick glasses.

"Why, sugarbun," said the lady, "what you want is a big plate of fudge instead."

"What else can you do?" said a dark-haired boy of about ten. "Do you read to children, or take them on picnics?"

"Well, picnics are one of my specialties: Big baskets of fried chicken and soft biscuits, cold chocolate milk, and coconut cream pies—anything you like, honey," said the lady. "But I don't enjoy reading much unless it is cookbooks. Do you enjoy hearing new recipes?"

"Not much, I guess," said the boy.

Elizabeth, Jenny, and Harry took one of the warm, crunchy cookies.

"I want her," said Harry.

"Wait till we've seen them all," said Jenny.

"Let's go to the information booth and see how you get one," said Elizabeth.

Inside the information booth were two boys of about twelve or thirteen.

"What can we do for you?" said one.

"We want to get one of these mothers," said Jenny.

"Did you bring one to trade in?" asked the boy.

"We don't have one, only a housekeeper," said Elizabeth.

"A wicked one," said Harry.

"Ordinarily, a trade is requested," said the boy. "To keep the supply steady, you know. We have a few mothers that come in without children, but not many. In any case, we can't let you take one out unless you get rid of the housekeeper. We've found it never works otherwise."

"What shall we do, then?" said Elizabeth. "We can't get rid of Mrs. Hinchley."

"The Gloom," said Harry.

"My assistant here specializes in advice for this kind of problem. He'll be able to help you," said the boy. "Hey, Edward, can you help these kids here? They're stuck with a housekeeper."

"What is she like?" said Edward. "You have to deal with them individually."

"Well," said Elizabeth, "she's terribly neat and clean, and she always wants everything in its right place."

"She never smiles and she never forgets anything," said Harry.

"She thinks everyone should be organized," said Jenny.

"Oh, yes," said Edward. "I know that kind. We've had them before. Just let me look it up."

He took down an old leather-bound notebook from a shelf nearby and leafed through it.

"Here we are," he said. " 'Efficient House-keepers'—now just a second while I read this. Some of the ideas here are hopelessly out-of-date. These records are at least two hundred years old."

"You mean the Mummy Market has been here that long?" said Elizabeth.

"Well, not the way it is now," said the boy. "It used to be called the Parental Exchange, Female Division."

"Is there a Daddy Market?" asked Harry. "Can we go there, too?"

"You can go there instead," said the boy, "but our most important rule is that no one can go to both at once. It's always disastrous."

"We'd better get a mother first," said Elizabeth.

"They don't do half the business we do, anyway," said Edward, leafing through the notebook. "The turnover in fathers is very slow. Wait a minute. Here we are. The most successful solution to the kind of housekeeper you have is the bureaucratic one."

"What does that mean?" asked Elizabeth.

"Well, we have found that they think filling out official forms is terribly important. If you make the forms long enough and difficult enough, they will do almost anything it tells them to do at the end. We have been helped enormously by the Internal Revenue Department."

"What's that?" asked Jenny.

"Income tax," said Edward. "You confuse them by saying, 'Enter here and on line eighty-two b, schedule K, the sum of the division of two per cent of line thirty-nine, page three.' Lots of stuff like that. None of them have ever caught on. They eventually decide that it isn't worth it to be a housekeeper, and they take up some other kind of work."

"Oh," said Elizabeth, who hadn't understood very well.

"If, after we interview your housekeeper, we decide that she might be just what some children want, we'll let her set up a stall here," said Edward. "You'd be surprised at the kind of mother some kids will pick, and we try to accommodate all kinds here."

"But what about keeping your supply of mothers going, in case you don't want The Gloom?" asked Elizabeth.

"We get a few mothers who come in by themselves because they want some children. It will be all right," said Edward.

"Can we pick one today?" said Jenny.

"Well, you can choose one if you like, and ask her if she'll wait till next week for you, but I'm afraid I can't let you take one home till then. You can expect your housekeeper to pack up and leave next Thursday morning."

"Oh, thank you," cried Elizabeth gratefully.

"Will you please fill out this card, giving your names, ages, and address, and your housekeeper's name and approximate age?"

"Sure," said Elizabeth. "Is that all?"

"That's all," said Edward. "Thank you for your business; and don't be discouraged if you make a mistake in choosing your first mother. You can always come back and try again."

"Let's start next to the cookie-mother, and go right around," said Elizabeth.

"Okay," said Jenny happily.

The next stall was the one with the guitar-playing mother. Some children were singing "On Top of Old Smoky" with her when the Martins came up. She wore blue jeans and a plaid shirt, and was barefooted. Her booth was set up to look like a simple summer cottage. Navaho rugs were on the floor, and a fire was burning in the fireplace behind her. The song came to its end.

"Can you play 'I've Been Working on the Railroad'?" said Harry.

"I'd rather play you a beautiful Israeli song about peace and love," said the mother.

"Oh," said Harry sadly as the mother started singing a strange and lovely melody. Her voice was clear and true, and the children listened till the end.

"Do you teach children to play the guitar?" said Jenny.

"Oh, yes," said the mother. "Folk music is good for everyone. It teaches international friendship and a feeling for the hard lot of the workingman."

Harry, who had been planning to grow up to be a workingman, kicked the booth gently with his toe.

"Do you like to play with someone who plays the recorder?" asked Jenny.

"That would be great fun," said the mother.

"Do you know 'I owe my soul to the company store'?" said a tall boy with long hair.

"Yes," said the mother, and started singing again.

"I want her," whispered Jenny.

"Oh, no!" said Harry. "She's horrible. I like that cookie one."

"Let's go on and see some more," said Elizabeth.

The next stall had curtains pulled across it, and a sign was pinned on them that said TAKEN.

The children stopped at the stall beyond it, and stared at its occupant with amazement.

She was tall and slender, and her face was surrounded by a cloud of golden hair. She wore black velvet lounging pajamas, and leaned against a pale-green satin couch.

"She's terribly beautiful," whispered Elizabeth.

The walls of her stall were covered with gold brocade, and a crystal chandelier hung overhead. She was smoking a cigarette in a long black holder, and she knocked its ash gracefully into an ashtray on a fragile table nearby.

Nobody dared say anything for a minute, and then Elizabeth said, "Do you really like children?"

"Of course I do, darling," said the beautiful lady.

"Why?" said Harry, scowling.

"They're so charming," said the lady. "They are the most priceless ornaments of the home."

"What do you do with them?" asked Elizabeth.

"With a little girl your age, I should have such fun. I would teach you how to dress to your best advantage. We should have to do something about your hair. You are getting much too old for braids—I'm sure Henri, my hairdresser, could do wonders for you."

"He could?" said Elizabeth breathlessly.

"Of course, my dear. He's an artist. I would certainly change your brother's wardrobe, too. He shouldn't be out in the city in old blue jeans and sneakers. A little suit with an Eton collar and short pants would be darling on him."

"I don't want one," said Harry crossly.

"Well, perhaps we shouldn't suit each other, young man," said the lady, drawing on her cigarette thoughtfully.

"Come on, Elizabeth. Let's go see the next one," said Harry.

Jenny started on and Elizabeth ran up to her.

"I liked her the best so far," she said. "It's too bad she thought she and Harry wouldn't suit each other. Why did you have to be rude to her, Harry?"

"I hate her," said Harry. "I want the cookie one."

"She's stupid," said Jenny. "The guitar one is the best one."

"I hate her, too," said Harry. "She doesn't like railroads and workingmen."

"Well, it's almost five o'clock," said Elizabeth. "If we don't find someone soon, we'll have to keep The Gloom."

The next stall was decorated like a cozy living-room. A braided rug was on the floor, simple maple furniture was scattered around.

Over the mantelpiece was a cross-stitch sampler that said:

GOD BLESS OUR HAPPY HOME

Seated in a comfortable armchair with a ruffled pink slipcover was a pleasant-looking woman in a light blue dress. Her round and dimpled face was bent over her sewing, but she looked up smiling as the children came up.

"Hullo, there," she said.

"Hullo," said Elizabeth. "What are you making?"

"Doll clothes for a little girl I know," said the mother.

"Do you teach children how to sew?" asked Jenny.

"Yes, sweetheart."

"What are those pink flowers?" said Harry, pointing to a vase of spiky blossoms.

"They're gladiolas," said the mother, "but I call them glads, because it is such a happy name."

"She sounds like Mrs. Cavour," whispered Harry to Jenny. "Do you make cookies and cake, too?" he asked.

"Of course, darling," she said. "I try to be a real home-type mommy."

"Do you read to children?" asked Elizabeth.

"Yes, I certainly do. I have a copy of *Little Lord Fauntleroy* right here with me."

"Do you sing with children and teach them new songs?" asked Jenny.

"Oh, I think that a group of children singing round the fire in the evening is one of the sweetest things there is."

"Just a minute. We'll be right back," said Elizabeth.

The children walked out into the center of the Square, where they could talk unheard.

"I like her," said Harry. "She's even nicer than the cookie one."

"I think she's nice, too," said Jenny. "If I can't have the guitar one."

"She's kind of sweetie-sweetie, don't you think?" said Elizabeth. "And she reads *Little Lord Fauntleroy*."

"Oh, he isn't so bad," said Jenny.

"Ten minutes to closing time," came a loud voice over an amplifier.

"Ten minutes to closing time."

"Oh, all right," said Elizabeth, "let's try her. She's better than The Gloom, anyway."

They went back to the home-type mummy, and there was an uncomfortable silence while they wondered what was the proper thing to say.

"Would you like to be our mother?" asked Jenny finally.

"That would be lovely. I'll come right with you. Just let me tidy up a bit."

"We can't take you till next week," said Elizabeth. "We have a mean housekeeper, and the rule is that she has to go first. Would you mind waiting till next Thursday?"

"Why you poor little things," said the mother. "Of course, I'll wait. I'll come right to your house if you'll tell me where you live."

"We live at twenty-two Ash Street, in Westville," said Elizabeth. "You can catch a bus in Revere Square."

"I'll be there in time for lunch, then, sweethearts," said the mother. "We'll have such a cozy time together. Good-bye till then."

CHAPTER 4

The Gloom's Departure

During the week that followed, the children were beset with many worries. Would The Gloom really leave? Edward had seemed very sure of his "bureaucratic" solution, but the children were not at all convinced. Would the new mother really come? Would she come while The Gloom was still there? If so, what would they say to The Gloom? Suppose The Gloom left and the new mother never showed up? What would they do then? The children discussed these problems in their tree house, but only succeeded in worrying each other more.

The time dragged. On Friday, they had a good game of kickball with the children in their neighborhood. Their rules were that people under five could be on both teams, so that they could always be up and always kick home runs, which were never counted in the score. People under seven were evenly divided between teams, and were always allowed to get to first base. Even the excitement of a game with a score of 39 to 37 had not been enough to lift the anxiety completely.

On Saturday, The Gloom received a thick and official-looking envelope in the mail. After she had opened it, she scowled at the wall for a while, and then told the children to go upstairs

and not to come down until their rooms were spotless, and on no account to interrupt her. When she called them to lunch, she was still scowling.

The children, thinking it was wisest to leave her alone, retreated to the tree house. Elizabeth and Jenny tried to distract themselves and Harry by reading. Elizabeth was reading *Treasure Island*, and Jenny was reading aloud to Harry from her favorite book of Russian fairy tales: " 'In Russia, the most common variety of witches are called babayaga witches. They have teeth of steel and live in little houses that revolve on chicken's feet.' "

"Elizabeth," said Jenny, "do you think The Gloom is a babayaga witch? That may be why she is so fussy about brushing teeth and things."

Elizabeth laughed. "Maybe if Edward really makes her go away, she'll be more cheerful," she said. "She can live in a little house on chicken feet instead of a regular one."

At supper time, The Gloom was anything but cheerful. She frowned steadily all during the meal.

"Is something the matter, Mrs. Hinchley?" asked Elizabeth innocently. "Can we help?"

The children leaned forward, hardly breathing with excitement.

"It is nothing to do with children. Only adults can understand matters of this kind," said The Gloom. "Elizabeth, I must ask you to see that Jennifer and Harrington brush their teeth thoroughly and scrub themselves well in the bath. I have some important paper work to do this evening, and I must not be disturbed."

"Yes, Mrs. Hinchley," said Elizabeth.

In the morning, The Gloom was even more distracted. After breakfast she announced that she would have to spend the day in her room, working on her papers. "You will have to get your own lunch," she said, "and if Harrington insists on having marshmallow fluff in his peanut-butter sandwich, please make sure that he eats it outdoors. I do not want to come down and find my kitchen all sticky."

"Yes, Mrs. Hinchley," said Elizabeth.

By afternoon, The Gloom had begun talking to herself. It was Harry, who had gone upstairs to feed his iguana lizard, who first heard her. He called his sisters, and they all listened outside her door. Not one of them felt a single pang of

conscience. They were all grinning with pleasure instead.

"You've always been perfectly competent,
Eunice Hinchley," The Gloom was saying. "All
you need do is follow the directions." A rustling
of papers could be heard, and then she began
talking again.

" 'Enter the number of children on line seven
of schedule D.' Yes. That's easy. Just write down
three. 'Then subtract the boys from the girls,

and enter fifty per cent of that on line twelve of page one.' Oh, dear. Take away Harrington; that leaves Elizabeth and Jennifer. But which fifty per cent do I enter? Elizabeth? Or Jennifer? Oh dear, oh dear."

There was silence for a while, and then she groaned aloud.

"I cannot do it. It's impossible. 'Amortization of emergency storage facilities. List all supplies used during the full term of your employment.' Number of jars of peanut butter, number of cans of tuna fish, etc. I give up. I give up completely. No profession is worth this agony." Silence followed, and the children retreated downstairs.

Later in the afternoon, The Gloom reappeared. "Elizabeth," she said. "I want you to mail this letter for me at once. I am sorry to say that I am resigning my job, but unforeseen circumstances have forced me to come to that decision. The new Social Security regulations concerning housekeepers have proved beyond my capacity."

"When are you leaving?" said Jenny.

"On Thursday, at seven A.M.," said The

Gloom. "A replacement will be sent to you the same day. The regulations are very clear on that point, although completely obscure on others. Please go along with the letter. You have just time to get it in the mailbox before the collection."

"I'll come too," said Harry.

"We'll all go," said Jenny.

They all smiled with satisfaction as the letter disappeared down the slot.

"Whee," said Jenny, "Edward was right. It worked." And quietly she began to sing:

> Ta-ra-ra boom de-ay
> The Gloom will go away
> And so we sing Hurray
> Ta-ra-ra boom de-ay.

CHAPTER 5

The Home-Type Mummy

On Thursday, the children made themselves breakfast after The Gloom had left, and to celebrate, they had whatever they felt like eating.

Elizabeth had root beer and a cucumber sandwich. Jenny had a fried egg covered with ketchup, and a cup of instant coffee. Harry had a marshmallow-fluff-and-Bosco sandwich and a Coca-Cola. They had to go to the store for the root beer and Coke, because The Gloom had never allowed them in the house, on the advice of the dentist.

After breakfast, they worked hard cleaning the kitchen and making beds to have the house nice for their new mother. It seemed she would never come. Harry's trucks bored him, Jenny couldn't finish a tune on her recorder, and Elizabeth couldn't read the next chapter of *Treasure Island*.

Finally, the doorbell rang. The children ran to open the door, and there stood the mother with a big suitcase.

"Hullo, children," she said. "What an adorable house you have."

"Come in," said Elizabeth politely.

"Thank you, sweetheart," said the mother. "Will you show me where my room is?"

The children led the way to the room The Gloom had slept in. It had white walls, a white spread on the bed, and straight white curtains. The rug was a light grey, and the bureau was painted white.

"Dearie me," said the mother. "This isn't cozy at all." She opened her suitcase and took out the sampler that said GOD BLESS OUR HAPPY HOME, and hung it on a nail in the wall where The Gloom had had a picture of Louis Pasteur. Then, while the children stared in amazement, she took out her bouquet of gladiolas still in their vase, and set it on the bureau.

"Didn't they get squashed in the suitcase?" said Harry.

"No, dear, these aren't real ones. They are the very best plastic kind. I think they're much nicer because they never wilt."

"Oh," said Harry.

"I'll have to do something about this room at the store tomorrow, but now let's get acquainted," said the mother. "Why don't you call me Mimsey. Don't you think that's a sweet name?"

"Okay, Mimsey," said Harry. Elizabeth and Jenny looked at each other in alarm.

Mimsey made them a good lunch, and the afternoon passed happily in showing her around the house. She was appreciative of everything except for Michael, Harry's iguana lizard, who, she said, was a nasty creature for such a sweet little boy to have. The only other incident which troubled the first day was at bedtime, when Jenny asked her to read her book of Russian fairy tales.

"Stories about witches and giants aren't good for children," said Mimsey. "They might frighten you, or give you bad dreams. I'd rather read a really nice book. I brought a copy of *The Water Babies* with me, specially to read to you. You'll love Mrs. Do-as-you-would-be-done-by."

At breakfast the next morning, Jenny and Harry reached for the last piece of bacon at the same moment. Jenny was faster, and grabbed it first.

"I wanted it," said Harry. "You're greedy, Jenny."

"Harry," said Mimsey, "we don't call names like that."

"I am not," said Jenny. "You just always want your own way."

"Jenny!" said Mimsey, in a shocked voice. "You must share with your brother, and neither of you must have feelings like that." She took the piece of bacon, and divided it in half. "There," she said. "You must learn to keep your hearts free from selfishness all the time."

That afternoon, Mimsey told the children to play happily while she went shopping. "I'll bring you all some lovely surprises," she said.

When she returned, loaded with packages, the children met her joyfully.

"The surprises come last, sweethearts," she

said. "Let me show you the cute things I bought for our home." A huge shopping bag turned out to hold some ruffled pink curtains, and a pink satin cushion with a hand-painted picture of a thatched cottage in a flower garden. Mimsey held it at arm's length and smiled with delight.

"Now for the surprises," she said. She handed a large package to each of the children. When Elizabeth opened hers, she found a Tiny Tears doll; and the other packages held a bride doll for Jenny and a groom doll for Harry.

"So the dolls can have their own happy family," said Mimsey, beaming.

The children thanked her politely, but that afternoon in the tree house they discussed their presents more frankly.

"Sally Greenbaum has a jackknife she found," said Harry. "I bet she'd trade it for the groom doll."

"You can't do that," said Elizabeth. "You'd hurt Mimsey's feelings. What am I going to do with a baby doll? But we have to keep them, and pretend we like them."

"Why did she have to get a bride doll?" said Jenny. "I wanted that camping set at Samson's Hardware Store so much."

"Well, I don't see what we can do about it," said Elizabeth. "She meant to be as nice as she could."

On Saturday, Johnny and Suzy Rabinowitz, who had come over to play, went home in disgust, taking Joe, their collie, with them because Mimsey had come rushing out waving a mop crying, "Oh, don't let that big, hairy brute frighten my children."

At supper, when Harry put a mayonnaise jar with four inchworms and a lilac twig in it by his place, Mimsey jumped up from her chair.

"Harry," she said, "take those awful worms outdoors right now. And remember, dear, it isn't kind to them to keep them in a jar."

The next afternoon, Jenny came in with a skinned knee and a torn dress. "Will you put a Band-Aid on this, Mimsey?" she said.

"Oh, you poor darling," said Mimsey. And with a shaking hand, she washed the scrape. "How did it happen?"

"I was trying to walk along the top of Sally's fence," said Jenny, "and I slipped."

Mimsey gasped. "You must promise me never to do that again," she said.

"But Sally's always doing it," said Jenny.

"She's really good at it."

"If her mother lets her do such dangerous things, I'll have to ask you not to play with her anymore, dear," said Mimsey.

On Monday, Mimsey went too far. She said to the children that she had asked Mr. Antonelli, the carpenter, to build them a little playhouse in the yard because it frightened her to have them climbing so high in that great big tree.

"We don't want a playhouse," said Elizabeth. "We like our tree house."

"Oh, you'll see how lovely it is when he makes it," said Mimsey. "He's coming on Friday, and he'll tear down that dangerous contraption in the tree, too."

"Oh, no, no!" cried all the children.

"Darlings," said Mimsey gently, "it is all settled. You don't want to frighten your Mimsey, do you?" She went on with her ironing, turning a smiling face to all entreaties, and she could not be swayed from her drastic plan.

The next morning, right after breakfast, the children took their problem to Mrs. Cavour. Her garden was much the same, but the roses were blooming—red, white, and pink. The irises were gone, but in their place the first color was

showing on the tall spires of delphiniums. They found her leaning against the sundial with a worried look on her face.

"Hullo, Mrs. Cavour. What's the matter?" said Elizabeth.

"It just doesn't seem right," she said, "but I'm afraid I shall have to use strong measures against the johnny-jump-ups. They want the whole garden to themselves. But tell me, did you find the Mummy Market?"

Luckily, Mrs. Cavour was able to sort out the confused story the children told her, interrupting one another as they told of the market and the success of Edward's plan to get rid of unwanted housekeepers and of the arrival of the home-type mummy.

"But now she's worse than The Gloom," said Harry. "She's going to tear down our tree house."

"Because it's too dangerous for her little lambs," mimicked Jenny.

"The terrible thing is that she tries to be so nice," said Elizabeth, "so we can't be mean to her, and yet she keeps doing awful things."

"We thought she'd be like you," said Harry, "because she had some flowers and she said she called them glads because it's such a happy name."

"Ah, yes," said Mrs. Cavour. "I see the picture. You mustn't be discouraged. I think you could have chosen a much worse mother on your first try. Only experience will help you find the right one. But I can see how difficult she must be for you. My grandfather always used to tell me '*Cave eos qui gladiolos amant*,' which means 'Watch out for people who like gladioli!' Well, now, let's see—when is this carpenter coming?"

"On Friday," said Elizabeth.

"Well, that's easy, then," said Mrs. Cavour. "Take her back to the Mummy Market on Thursday, and call the carpenter and tell him you are sorry but he won't be needed."

"But how can we tell her? It will break her heart if we say we don't want her," said Elizabeth.

"I don't believe she'll be as upset as you think," said Mrs. Cavour. "She sounds as if one family of children was much the same to her as another. But if it worries you, perhaps we can work out a plan." She watched a bee at a foxglove for a moment while she thought.

"I think the best plan would be to unsettle her a

bit, first, and then launch an all-out attack. Why don't you spend the day here? Goodness knows I can use you. The rose bugs are worse this June than they have been for fifteen years, and I expect the Japanese beetles any day now. They're almost as regular as the warblers in their appearance. As for your Mimsey, you'll find that she is sufficiently unsettled when you return. And now for the attack. Don't you have a Gila monster, Harry?"

"He's an iguana," said Harry.

"Oh, of course," said Mrs. Cavour. "Well, I think that if you tell her, sometime tomorrow, that he has escaped and ask her to help you find him, you will have no further trouble."

The children had a beautifully peaceful day at Mrs. Cavour's, where the only sweetness was the fragrance of the flowers. For lunch, they had homemade bread and honey, milk and strawberries, and all day long, all the raw peas they wanted. Late in the afternoon, when the sunlight in the garden seemed to grow more luminous as the shadows grew cooler, they started for home. As they came down Ash Street they saw that a police car was parked in front of their house. They came in quietly, and heard Mimsey's voice.

"But they are so young," she was sobbing. "Something terrible may have happened to them."

"Now lady, calm down," said a deep voice.

They came into the living room and found Mimsey, her face mottled with tears, and a tall policeman holding his hat in his hands.

"Oooh," shrieked Mimsey, collapsing in a chair when she saw them.

"There now, lady, what did I tell you?" said the policeman. "Kids are kids. You've got to expect a few high-jinks." His face became severe, and he said, "You children shouldn't go off like that without telling your mother; she was worried sick about you."

"Where have you been," cried Mimsey, rushing toward them, arms outstretched. "You naughty lambs; you frightened your poor Mimsey so."

The policeman fled, leaving the children to comfort their poor Mimsey.

They went to bed that night having succeeded in comforting her only partially, and feeling a bit guilty but pleasantly excited about the plan for tomorrow—like heroic traitors.

"We can't really let him go," said Harry the next day. "He'd get lost for sure—he isn't very smart."

"Let's get a cardboard box and punch some holes in it for him and put him in the attic," said Elizabeth.

This was soon done, and then they went downstairs and told Mimsey.

"Michael is lost," said Harry.

"What?" said Mimsey. "One of your little playmates? That's just what I thought had happened to you yesterday. How terrible for his poor mother."

"Michael is Harry's iguana," said Elizabeth.

"His what?" said Mimsey.

"His lizard, that you said was a nasty creature," said Jenny.

"Oh, no," cried Mimsey.

"Will you please help me find him?" said Harry.

"He hasn't had his breakfast yet," said Jenny.

"Not in the house," said Mimsey. "That creature isn't lost in the house, is it?"

"Yes," said Harry. "I was just smoothing him gently, and he got away."

"Where?" asked Mimsey.

"In my room," said Harry, "but he's not there anymore. We looked everywhere."

"He's not in Jenny's room or mine, either," said Elizabeth. "Would you help us look in your room, please?"

"In my room?" said Mimsey, her voice rising higher. "Do you think it's in my room?"

"Well, we don't think he could go down the stairs," said Elizabeth. "Please come and help."

Mimsey swallowed, and using all the courage in her meager supply, she said, "All right. I'll come with you."

They looked under the bed, and behind the pink cushion. They looked in the closet, and then Jenny said, "There he is; I see him." With a speed surprising in someone who is frightened of climbing trees, Mimsey leaped onto the bureau, knocking down the sampler that said *God Bless Our Happy Home*.

"Oh, no, it was just a shoe," said Jenny.

Mimsey wilted with relief.

"There he is, under the radiator," shouted Elizabeth.

"Oh, he's climbing up the bureau," said Jenny.

Mimsey screamed and gave a flying leap, like an orangutan, and landed on the bed, knocking off the pink cushion. Her face was pale, and she was breathing rapidly. The children took pity on her.

"No, he seems to be gone now," said Elizabeth.

Naturally, although the children hunted all day, they were unable to find Michael. Mimsey passed a sleepless night, sitting up in her bed with the light on. In the morning, the children found her, red-eyed and with a drawn face, packing her suitcase.

"You must forgive your Mimsey, darlings," she said sadly, "but I cannot stay in the house any longer with that creature loose in it. I shall have to go back to the Mummy Market and find some other little children, who don't keep monsters in their bedrooms. You won't have any trouble. There is some cold chicken in the icebox and tapioca pudding for dessert. You will easily find another mummy at the market; but for goodness' sake, warn her that she's coming to a house with a monster loose in it. I will leave you the curtains and the pretty pink cushion to remember me by." And, after hugging and kissing them tearfully, she said good-bye and left them.

They brought Michael down from the attic and told him that they would always be grateful to him for saving their tree house. Then they called Mr. Antonelli and told him he wouldn't be needed, and after lunch they washed their hands and faces and prepared to go shopping for a new mother.

CHAPTER 6

Eeny-Meeny-Miney-Moe

At the Mummy Market the children saw that the cookie-mother was back again, but the guitar-mother and the beautiful lady were missing. Mimsey was there, back in the same cozy stall, and she smiled pleasantly at them as they passed.

"Well, at least we know what to avoid now," said Elizabeth. "I bet the children who took the cookie one got sick of her, too."

They went and thanked Edward, at the information booth, for getting rid of The Gloom so successfully, and told him that their first mother hadn't worked out very well.

"Everybody makes mistakes the first few times," said Edward kindly. "Just keep trying, and you'll get what you want eventually." He turned to help another customer, and the children went to look at the mothers on display.

The first one they came to was the piano-playing one they had noticed on their first visit to the market. Her stall was almost entirely filled with a huge concert grand piano. She was older than Mimsey, and she was wearing a dress of flowing grey silk. Huge piles of music books were stacked in the corners of the stall. A marble bust of Beethoven was on a small table in the

only space left by the piano. The children listened politely while she finished playing.

"Do you teach children to play the piano?" asked Jenny.

"Oh, yes," she said. "I love to play four hands with children, but I like them to learn another instrument as well; then we can have more chamber music."

"I play the recorder," said Jenny.

"Come on, Jenny," said Harry.

"Hush up," said Jenny.

"Do your brother and sister play?" said the mother.

"No," said Jenny.

"Too bad," said the mother, "but maybe it's just as well. I am hoping to find a family of four children for a string quartet. Imagine the *Trout Quintet* performed all in the family." She sighed happily.

"Well, good-bye," said Jenny. "I hope you find them."

"Thank you, dear," said the mother.

The next stall had a great many children in front of it, talking earnestly with the mother. She had long braids twisted around her head, and she wore tortoise shell glasses. Her stall was crowded with all kinds of wonderful things. In one corner, a complicated apparatus of test tubes and rubber hoses was hissing over a Bunsen burner. In another, an easel was set up ready for painting. A table covered with strange-looking cans was in the center of the stall.

"Creativity," she was saying to the children, "is the important thing."

"What are you making in the chemistry set?" asked a boy in a striped T-shirt.

"I'm not making anything," she answered. "It is there for intellectual stimulation. That is the greatest gift we mothers can give our children."

"What is?" said Harry.

"Intellectual stimulation," said the mother.

"It's probably something like a groom doll," whispered Harry to Jenny.

"What are these things for?" asked Jenny, pointing to the things on the table.

"This is a potter's wheel, and these cans contain clay. Here is the real mud of creation," said the mother, lovingly patting one of the cans.

"I bet she's a teacher just looking for some children to bother during the summer," whispered Elizabeth. "Let's look at the next one."

From their position at the back of the crowd of children, they looked over at the next stall

63

and were startled to see that its occupant was The Gloom. She was in a white and spotless kitchen, washing the shining floor. Two little girls in torn and dirty dresses were listening to her with interest. "Cleanliness is next to godliness," she was saying.

"Let's get out of here," said Jenny.

They retreated back past the piano mother, and ran across the square to the row of booths on the other side. They passed by a bare stall with no decoration at all, only a woman sitting in a chair, and went straight to a stall surrounded by children of all sizes.

A small tent was pitched in the stall, and in front of it a campfire was burning. A large young woman in khaki shorts was toasting marshmallows over the fire and handing them out to the children.

"Do you really take kids on camping trips?" said a girl wearing a girl scout uniform.

"As often as you like," said the mother. "I can't get too much of the outdoors, and I love doing things with kids."

"What other things do you do with them?" asked a boy in a black motorcycle jacket.

"Oh, all kinds of things. Baseball, touch football, fishing, hiking, cookouts, bird walks. I bet you'd like go-cart racing. I have great fun doing all kinds of sports with children."

"Can you cook?" said Harry.

"If you've never tasted my steak and corn on the cob cooked over a campfire, you don't know what eating is," said the mother, rubbing her hands.

"Do you like singing?" asked Jenny.

"You bet I do," said the mother. "Round the campfire after a good dinner, there's nothing like a rousing song."

"Do you read to children?" asked Elizabeth.

"Oh, my, yes," said the mother. "Sharing the good old adventure yarns with children is great fun. *Treasure Island, The White Company, King Arthur and His Knights, Robin Hood*—all of them. Here, have a marshmallow."

"Thank you," said Elizabeth.

"Can I have one, too? I want one. Me, too," shouted many voices.

The Martins retreated slightly to discuss the out-of-doors mother. Elizabeth generously gave her marshmallow to Harry.

"What do you think of her?" she asked.

"I think she's nifty," said Jenny. "Nothing

sweetie-sweetie about her; she wouldn't give you a bride doll or tear down your tree house."

"She's kind of funny, though," said Harry. "More like someone's father than their mother."

"Don't you want her?" asked Elizabeth.

"I guess so," said Harry. "She's better than Mimsey."

"Okay. We'll ask her, then," said Elizabeth. They turned back to the mother, who was putting a new marshmallow on her stick.

"We'd like it if you'd be our mother," said Elizabeth politely.

"No, I want her," said the girl scout.

"I want her, too," said the boy in the motor-cycle jacket. "It's not fair."

"Let's count out like good sports," said the mother.

> Eeny-meeny-miney-moe,
> Catch a tiger by the toe,
> If he hollers, let him go.
> Out goes Y-O-U.

And she pointed to the boy in the motorcycle jacket. He went off kicking the cobblestones with his black boots. The girl scout tightened her lips and glared at Elizabeth.

66

Eeny-meeny-miney-moe,
Catch a tiger by the toe,
If he hollers, let him go.
Out goes Y-O-U.

And she pointed at the girl scout. "Be a good scout, and better luck next time," she said. "And now, I'll be right with you," she said to Elizabeth. "Just let me put out my campfire. That's one of the first rules of the woods—always make sure your fire is completely out before leaving camp." She got a bucket of sand from behind the tent, dumped it on the fire, and stamped on it. "There we are," she said. She went into the tent and came out with an enormous knapsack, and swinging it to her shoulders, she jumped down from her booth and started off with the children.

CHAPTER 7

Mom

They reached home rather hot and tired, because their new mother had insisted that they get off the bus and walk the last mile. "I can't let you get soft," she said.

In spite of their fatigue, they were delighted with her. She had told them to call her Mom, and had told them the names of all the trees and birds they had seen on their walk.

When they took her to her room, she said, "We'll have to get rid of these awful things," and to their great satisfaction, she took the pink cushion off the bed and gave it to Elizabeth to put in the attic. She opened the windows wide, and ripped down the ruffled curtains. "Can't have this nonsense between me and the out-doors," she said. "Now I can settle in." She opened her knapsack and took out a large framed photograph of a group of young women in baggy sweat suits, and hung it on the nail where Mimsey's sampler had been. "That's my college field-hockey team," she said. "The year I was center forward, we were undefeated." On the bureau, she arranged a pair of stuffed scarlet tanagers.

"Taxidermy is my hobby," she said. "I consider these my masterpieces."

She looked at her watch. "No time to do much today," she said. "Let's have a cookout in the backyard for supper." The children enjoyed the evening immensely—the hamburgers were delicious, and they had big slices of watermelon for dessert. Mom divided them into teams—Jenny and Elizabeth against her and Harry for a watermelon-seed fight; and then she read them *Treasure Island* until bedtime.

The next morning, at six o'clock, the children woke to hear Mom shouting, "Hit the deck, kids. The sun's been up for hours." The children mumbled drowsily, rolled over, and went back to sleep. She came and shook them, saying, "Only dudes and softies sleep late in the morning." So they struggled out of bed, and were glad that they had when they saw how bright the day was, and started on the griddle cakes that Mom had made for breakfast.

"This morning we'll have to equip you all for camping," she said. "Let's make a list. You need sleeping bags, knapsacks, ponchos, hatchets, canteens, and knives. You won't need a tent in the summer; the open air is better for you."

"There's a nifty camping set at Samson's Hardware Store," said Jenny. "It's a belt with hooks on it, and it has a leather pouch and a flashlight and a little canteen and a jackknife hanging on it."

"That's kid stuff," said Mom. "I'm going into an army surplus store and get you the real thing."

"Oh," said Jenny.

"You kids pack a lunch and ride your bikes out to the country for the day, and I'll meet you here at five o'clock. I'll get a big steak, too, and we'll have a real feast tonight."

"Boy, who could have ever traded her in?" said Elizabeth as they sat by a small brook, eating lunch. The day passed as summer days should: full of peace and sun and a good dinner at the end of it. Only one thing marred its perfection. When Mom was tucking them in at bedtime she said, "That's a really nice iguana you have there, Harry. We'll have to get you a mate for it, and you can breed them."

"Oh, no thanks, Mom," said Harry, politely. "Michael's plenty. Sometimes I even forget to feed *him*, and I don't want to have a whole lot."

"Nonsense," said Mom. "If we get too many, we can stuff some of them. I'll teach you how."

Harry turned pale. Elizabeth came to his rescue.

"Stuff Michael's children!" she cried. "We couldn't do that ever."

"Oh, well, then, have it your own way," said Mom briskly. "I see I have to toughen you up a bit before you'll be real sportsmen."

On Saturday, Mom's purchases were delivered, and the children were delighted with them. Mom took them on a picnic and taught them how to use their hatchets, and how to make willow whistles with their new knives.

"Speaking of whistles," she said, "I've got a great idea. You know that little whistle you're always fooling with, Jenny?"

"You mean my recorder?" said Jenny.

"I guess that's what you call it," said Mom. "Well, do you know how to play taps and reveille?"

"I could figure it out, I guess," said Jenny.

"I want you to be our bugler, then," said Mom. "I'll wake you a few minutes before the others, and you can play reveille for us."

"I don't want to get up any earlier than the others," said Jenny.

"Nonsense. That's an order," said Mom. "Buglers never mind losing a little sleep. Now, you be sure and bring it when we go camping, too. We'll go tomorrow."

That night, Jenny had to stand in the hall after Elizabeth and Harry were tucked in, and play taps; she had tried to do it sitting up in bed, but Mom had said, "Stand at attention when you play. When you do something, do it right."

"Elizabeth, give Harry back his sleeping bag. Campers must learn to carry their own equipment," said Mom as they struggled up the trail through the forest late Sunday afternoon.

"But he's tired. He's only six," said Elizabeth.

"We'll stop and rest, then," said Mom. "It's not much farther, anyway."

After a short stop, they shouldered their packs and climbed on up the hill.

"Here we are," said Mom as they came to a level space by a small stream. They were in a large grove of big white pines and hemlocks. The air was full of that truly summertime smell—sun on white pines; and the soft needles underfoot muffled the sound of their footsteps. The only noise was the gurgle of the little brook, and then, clear and lonesome, came the pure song of a wood thrush.

"I wish I had my bird traps," said Mom. "That's a wood thrush, and it's just what I need for my collection."

The children shuddered.

"Well, now, let's get to work and pitch camp," said Mom cheerfully. "Elizabeth, you and Jenny take your hatchets and cut some nice pine boughs for our beds. Harry, you can start gathering wood for the fire. I've brought us the biggest steak you ever saw."

The work was soon done—the sleeping bags spread out on their soft and fragrant beds, the fire burning, and the steak sizzling away.

"Isn't this the life?" asked Mom. "Give me the woods any day." And the children agreed with all their hearts. The dark came up and surrounded them, but they sat close to the warm red light from the fire and sang into the stillness while their marshmallows browned and blackened.

Mom banked up the fire, and they crawled into their sleeping bags. An owl answered Jenny when she played taps, and then silence fell. But only for a moment. Soon the whine of mosquitos filled their ears. They slapped and wiggled and slapped again.

"Mom, I can't go to sleep," said Harry. "The mosquitos keep biting me."

"Get down under your sleeping bag, then," said Mom.

"Then I get all sweaty," said Harry.

"If you're going to be a camper, you have to be a man, Harry," said Mom.

The mosquitos droned on. Then a new sound came. The patter of rain. "Spread your ponchos over your sleeping bags, and go to sleep," said Mom. Somehow *she* was able to sleep soundly through the rest of the night, but the children —wet and cold and miserable—only dozed, and woke and dozed again.

At breakfast, it was still raining. Wearing their ponchos like dark green ghosts, the children huddled around the hissing fire. Mom had carefully covered a supply of wood, like the good camper she was, to make sure of a hot breakfast.

After scrambled eggs, bacon, and hot coffee —even for Harry—they felt a little better. Even Mom didn't try to keep them out in the woods in the rain.

"We'll pack up and go home," she said, "but we'll be back as soon as the weather changes."

Tripping and stumbling, and aching with
fatigue, they started down the trail.

"Let's sing a rousing marching song to give
us some pep," said Mom, and she started singing:

> Tramp, tramp, tramp,
> The boys are marching.
> Cheer up, comrades, they will come. . . .
> In the prison cell I sit,
> Thinking, mother dear, of you
> And our sweet and happy home
> So far away. . . .

Elizabeth began to cry.

After a night's sleep in their own beds, the children were physically recovered from their camping trip, but none of them were looking forward to another one. It had stopped raining, but the children were glad to see that it was still cloudy. They spent most of the morning enjoying the peace of their tree house, and in the afternoon, the neighborhood children came for a kickball game in their backyard. Mom insisted on playing too. She took charge of dividing up the teams. She made Elizabeth captain of one, and herself of the other.

"We don't have captains; we just play," said Jenny.

"Well, then, it's high time you learned to do it right," said Mom. She put Lily Rabinowitz, Johnny, and Suzy's little sister, who was four, on Elizabeth's team, and Jimmy Nicholson, who was three but big for his age, on hers.

"We let people who are under five be on both sides because they like to be up better than in the field," said Elizabeth.

"If they're old enough to play, they're old enough to obey the rules," said Mom. "That little one there is too young to play." She pointed to Mitzy Greenbaum, who was two, and who had come over from next door with her sister Sally.

"Mitzy always plays," said Sally. "It's one of her favorite things."

"Well, I'm sorry," said Mom, "but this is no sport for a toddler."

"I won't play either, then," said Sally. "Come on, Mitzy, let's go home." She took her little sister by the hand, stuck out her tongue at Elizabeth, and walked proudly off.

"All right, now," said Mom. "Play ball. You take the field, Elizabeth, and we'll be up first. You pitch for your team and I'll pitch for mine."

The first one up was Jimmy Nicholson. Elizabeth rolled the ball gently, so that it came to a stop right in front of him. He gave it a little kick, and started running for first base. Elizabeth picked up the ball and pretended to trip, landing on her stomach and losing the ball. Jimmy's team was shouting, "Run, Jimmy, run." Elizabeth threw the ball to Suzy Rabinowitz on first, who let it slip through her fingers, screaming, "Oh, darn it," as Jimmy sped on to second base. By the time Suzy had retrieved the ball, he had passed third and was heading for home. Suzy threw the ball wildly to her brother, the catcher, who caught it a split second after Jimmy had touched home plate.

"I made a home win," shouted Jimmy, happily.

"What a bunch of butterfingers," said Mom disgustedly.

By the time Elizabeth's team was up at bat, the score was 41 to 0, everyone was hot and cross, and Lily Rabinowitz was whining, "I want a turn; I want a turn." Every time Mom had come up, the bases had been loaded, and she had kicked the ball over the fence for a home run.

The first one up on Elizabeth's team was Harry. He stepped up to the plate, and Mom sent the ball whizzing by, almost knocking down Jenny, her catcher. "Strike one," called Mom.

Again the ball whizzed by, and Harry kicked, but the ball bounced backward for a foul. "Keep your eye on the ball," said Mom. "You can't hit it right if you don't watch it."

"Well, don't throw it so fast," said Harry.

"Nonsense," said Mom. "We must all play to win."

She hurled the ball again, and Harry kicked and missed.

"Three strikes and you're out," she shouted.

"You're not fair," said Harry. "That isn't the way Elizabeth pitched."

"Don't be a poor sport," said Mom.

The next one up was Lily Rabinowitz. She stood aside and watched with interest as the ball shot by three times. She still stood there after Mom shouted, "Out."

"Move over and let the next man up," said Mom.

"I didn't have my turn yet," said Lily.

"Yes, you did," said Mom.

"No, I didn't. I didn't have my home run," said Lily, calmly.

"If you're going to play, you have to do it right," said Mom. "Three strikes and you're out."

Lily began to cry.

"You're no fair," said Johnny. "She always gets a home run."

"Not unless she kicks it good and hard," said Mom.

"You're ruining it all," said Suzy. "Come on,

Lily, let's go over to Sally's house. We can play it the right way there."

"We'll come with you," said Jimmie's brother Chris. And all the other children followed.

The Martins found themselves alone in their yard listening to the shouts and laughter coming from the Greenbaum's. They fled to their tree house, carefully pulling up the rope ladder to keep out Mom.

"I hate her," said Harry. "She's mean."

"She sure is," said Jenny. "She makes Mimsey look good."

"We've got to get rid of her fast," said Elizabeth. "Let's go see Mrs. Cavour first thing to-morrow."

"You'd go right now if you had to play taps tonight," said Jenny.

"It would be getting dark before we got home," said Elizabeth.

"Okay. I guess I can do it one more night," said Jenny.

Right after breakfast, they went to see Mrs. Cavour. She listened attentively while they told of the horrors of living with Mom.

"What did we do wrong?" said Elizabeth. "We thought she was just the opposite of Mimsey, and she seemed wonderful at first."

"You made a very natural mistake," said Mrs. Cavour. "You thought that if she was interested in different things than Mimsey she would be a different kind of person; but really, down at their roots, they are the same."

"What do you mean, the same?" said Jenny. "There never was anybody more different."

Mrs. Cavour pinched a lemon verbena leaf between her fingers, and held it to her nose.

"You remember I told you that one family of children was very much the same to Mimsey as another?"

"Yes," said Jenny.

"What do you think someone who chooses her children by saying, 'Eeny-meeny-miney-moe,' feels?"

"Oh, I see what you mean," said Elizabeth.

"She doesn't really notice what you are like at all," said Mrs. Cavour. "That's why she does such terrible things like trying to stuff Michael's children. She isn't cruel; she just has no feelings, poor thing."

"She's not a poor thing," said Harry. "She's too tough."

"Well, then you won't worry about hurting her feelings when you tell her to go back to the Mummy Market," said Mrs. Cavour. "And I think you had better tell her at once; you need to have a quiet day by yourselves before you try another one."

"I'm kind of scared to try again," said Elizabeth. "They turn out so horrible."

"I think the mistake you make is that you are fooled by a lot of fancy trappings," said Mrs. Cavour. "Good mothers are often rather like zinnias: a bit ordinary but very dependable."

Back at the house, the children squared their shoulders and confronted Mom.

"We have to talk to you, man to man," said Jenny.

"Good," said Mom. "What about?"

"We feel that we don't suit each other, and you had better go back to the Mummy Market," said Elizabeth.

"Nonsense," said Mom. "We haven't had a real camping trip yet."

"We don't want one, either," said Harry.

"Don't chicken out now," said Mom. "We've hardly gotten off the ground."

"Be a good sport, Mom," said Elizabeth, "and obey the rules of the game."

"You're right," said Mom. "I'd never want it said that I'm a bad loser."

She went to her room and packed her knapsack. "So long, kids," she said, and strode off down the street.

"Better luck next time," Elizabeth called after her, and they all started giggling.

CHAPTER 8

"Do You Really Understand Children?"

The children went to bed early that night, and in the morning they slept late. They went downstairs and made breakfast and carried it upstairs and ate it in bed. They left the breakfast dishes unwashed until after lunch, and then, after partially straightening up the house, they left for the Mummy Market.

They saw no sign of Mimsey, and they hoped she had found a happy family of little lambs who were just right for her. The Gloom was missing, too, and they wondered who could possibly have picked her.

They passed the beautiful lady, who was back

again; and although Elizabeth wished she could know what wonders Henri would do with her hair, they didn't stop.

The next stall they came to had a large group of children in front of it and they were all laughing at something the mother had told them. Elizabeth, Jenny, and Harry stopped to listen. The mother was wearing a cotton dress with a gay print of elephants on it. Her stall was arranged like a playroom. A Ping-Pong table was in the center of it, and on shelves all around the walls were toys and games of all kinds. A game of Monopoly was laid out on the floor ready for playing.

"What animal can jump higher than a house?" she was saying.

"A kangaroo," said one voice.

"Wrong," said the mother.

"A rabbit, a deer, a horse, a squirrel." Many children were shouting answers.

"Wrong," said the mother. "All animals. A house can't jump at all."

"Do you play games with children all the time?" said a girl with yellow hair.

"Yes, indeed," said the mummy. "It's my idea of the jolliest fun there is. Let's play 'I packed my trunk to go to Grandmother's house.' I'll begin: I packed my trunk to visit Grandmother's house, and in it I put an ant-eater."

"I packed my trunk to go to Grandmother's house," said the girl with yellow hair, "and in it I put an anteater and a baseball."

"Come on, let's go," said Elizabeth. "She'd probably turn out to be an indoor Mom."

They continued down the line of stalls, stoping only briefly to examine the mothers. They passed one whose stall contained a Shetland pony, two Labrador retrievers, and assorted small animals. "All children should have pets," she was saying. Harry was tempted, but Elizabeth and Jenny pulled him on.

They didn't even bother to stop at the next one. Her stall contained shelves of wheat germ, yogurt, stone-ground whole wheat flour, powdered milk, and safflower oil. "The best thing we mothers can do for our children is give them strong healthy bodies," she was saying as they passed. On they went, finding no one whom they felt would be sure of noticing what they were like. They crossed the market square and passed Mom, surrounded by children. She waved at them, and they waved back and went on. They passed the mother in the bare stall, sitting in her chair.

"She looks nice," said Elizabeth, "let's stop and talk to her."

"Oh, come on, Elizabeth," said Jenny. "You can't tell anything about her, her stall's all empty."

Finally they came to a mother who seemed worth considering. Her stall was set up like a book-lined sitting room. A soft green rug was on the floor and a low leather couch was against the wall. She was wearing a straight blue skirt and a white blouse. Her light brown hair was pulled back in a bun, and she was sitting in a chair covered with flowered chintz.

"Why do you want children?" asked Elizabeth.

"Well, I feel that I can help them," said the mother pleasantly. "I understand children and their problems."

"Do you really understand children?" said Jenny.

"Yes," said the mother. "I have studied child psychology and read all the books on child development."

"Do you read to children, and things like that?" asked Elizabeth.

"Oh, yes. A feeling of comfortable friendship must be part of every parent-child relationship," said the mother.

"Do you like iguanas?" said Harry.

"That's a kind of lizard, isn't it?" said the mother. "Do you have one?"

"Yes," said Harry. "Do you like them?"

"Well, let's put it this way," said the mother. "I feel that every little boy should have a pet. It teaches responsibility."

"Do you like music?" asked Jenny. "Do you like singing?"

"I feel that any child with musical interests should be encouraged," said the mother. "It helps to develop a sense of personal identity."

"Oh," said Jenny.

The children walked on to get a chance to discuss this mother privately.

"What about her?" said Elizabeth. "Do you think she's what Mrs. Cavour meant?"

"She doesn't seem like much fun," said Jenny. "But I guess Mrs. Cavour knows what's the right kind to pick."

"What do you think, Harry," said Elizabeth.

"Well, she's ordinary okay and she says she understands children, so I guess she'll do," he said.

They went back to the understanding mother, and Elizabeth said, "Do you think you'd like to be our mother?"

"Oh, yes," said the mother, "but I feel that since I have special talents I should wait for children with deep emotional problems. You look like very undisturbed children to me."

"Oh, no," said Jenny, "we have terrible problems. We don't have any mother, and we can't seem to pick one that understands us."

"You probably need help in recognizing your own needs," said the mother. "All right. I see that I can be a great help to you. I'll come. You go ahead, and I'll join you later. I have to arrange to have my books sent out. Just tell me your address."

The children told her where they lived, and then went home, feeling that this time, at last, they had used their heads and chosen correctly.

CHAPTER 9

Babs

The children were waiting in the front yard when the new mother drove up in a taxi late in the afternoon. The driver put her suitcase and three cardboard cartons of books on the sidewalk, and then he opened the trunk and took out a large and magnificent doll house.

"Pretty lucky little girls," he said.

"Wow," said Jenny. "That's better than the one Suzy's grandmother gave her."

"Is it for us?" said Elizabeth.

"It isn't a toy," said the mother. "I use it in my work, but you may certainly play with it."

Elizabeth and Jenny looked at each other in baffled silence.

The cartons were too heavy to carry, so the children helped bring the books in by armloads.

"You can call me Babs," said the mother as they carried the last load up the stairs. "It's short for Barbara. I think it will be better if you think of me as a friend and don't call me mother."

When everything had been put in Babs's room, she opened her suitcase and took out a large painting. It was of a rough texture with wild colors clashing together in whirls and straggles. She hung it on the nail where Mom's hockey team had been.

"What's that?" said Harry.

"It's called 'The Human Child at Two and a Half,'" said Babs. "I painted it myself."

Babs fed them frozen chicken pie for dinner. "If I spend too much time cooking, I won't be able to devote myself to developing our relationship," she said.

The first days with Babs passed happily, if a little blandly, and the children were grateful for a calm life after Mom. Babs baffled them occasionally by asking them all, even Harry, to play with her doll house while she looked on and took notes. But when she explained that she was only trying to understand them better, the children humored her in her peculiar desires.

The first sign of real trouble came on Monday afternoon. Harry wanted to make a wheelbarrow out of a wooden box he had found, and he looked everywhere for a wheel that he had been saving from an old broken tricycle. Finally he asked Babs if she had seen it.

"Oh, I threw that out," she said.

"But it's mine, and I wanted it," said Harry.

"Children shouldn't be allowed to play with broken toys," said Babs. "They develop a careless attitude toward material possessions."

"It wasn't a broken toy. It was a perfectly good wheel," said Harry.

"Now, Harry," said Babs, "if I'm going to help you, I have to decide what's best for you."

"But it wasn't your wheel," shouted Harry. "It was mine, and I need it."

"I know what you need much better than you could, Harry," said Babs serenely.

"You do *not*, or you wouldn't throw away other people's things," said Harry, still shouting. "I think you're mean."

"That's right, Harry. Let it all out," said

Babs. "Let out the old mean feelings, and then there will be room for new good feelings."

Harry was frightened. "I hate you! I hate you!" he yelled.

"That's right, Harry," said Babs.

Harry ran out of the room, crying hard. He dashed blindly out of the house and across the yard to the tree house. He climbed up and pulled up the ladder and sat there by himself, watching the sun on the leaves.

"The Rose and the Sword Forever," called Elizabeth gently. There was no answer. "Hey, Harry, let me up."

"That's a stupid password, and I don't want to let you up," said Harry.

"I've got your wheel," said Elizabeth. "Jenny and I looked through the trash barrel for it."

"You did?" said Harry, sticking his head over the edge. "Oh, thanks. I'm sorry. Come on up." And he tossed down the rope ladder.

"What do you think is the matter with her?" said Jenny when they were all settled inside the tree house.

"She's stupid," said Harry.

"She's sort of crazy," said Elizabeth, "saying,

'That's all right,' when you say you hate her, and always watching us play in that nutty doll house."

"Do you suppose she'd say, 'That's all right,' no matter what we did?" said Jenny.

"Let's find out," said Elizabeth.

"Oh, boy!" said Harry.

"Let's be really bad, and see what she does," said Jenny.

They started off gradually. At dinner that night Jenny said, "I hate TV dinners. You're a bad cook."

"I explained that to you," said Babs. "If I spend all of my time cooking, I will be just a housewife, and I won't be able to be an intelligent mother to you all."

"Well, I won't eat it," said Jenny, and shutting her eyes to get more courage, she threw her plate on the floor.

"That's all right, dear," said Babs. "It's natural for you to reject me at first. Would you like a peanut butter sandwich instead?"

The next morning after breakfast Babs gave them each a hammer and took them out into the backyard and gave them some blocks of wood and some nails.

"Here, children," she said. "I see that your cross feelings are stronger than I had thought. Why don't you pound these nails into the wood, and if you like, you may pretend that the nail is someone you are cross at."

"You mean just pound nails and not make anything?" said Harry.

"Yes, Harry. It's to make you feel better," said Babs, and she went into the house to wash the breakfast dishes.

"Boy. Is this stupid," said Harry.

"Oh, I don't know," said Jenny. "Let's try. WHAM! That's Babs I'm whamming."

"WHAM," said Elizabeth. "Wham on you, Mom."

"WHAM on The Gloom. BOOM, BOOM," said Harry, pounding away.

The children enjoyed the hammering for a little while, but it soon lost its charm and grew boring.

"It makes me wish I could really wham someone," said Elizabeth.

"I know," said Jenny. "Let's go hammer up that crazy doll house."

"Oh," said Harry, "can we knock it all to bits?"

"Do you really dare?" asked Elizabeth.

"Sure," said Jenny, who wasn't quite telling the truth. "Sure, I dare. Come and watch me." Jenny couldn't back out now, but she told herself that she didn't care anyhow.

The children circled the house and snuck in at the front door. They went quietly up the stairs and into Babs's room.

They stood silent before the doll house for a minute, and then Jenny lifted her hammer and, WHAM, down went the chimney. Elizabeth and Harry started pounding too. They smashed the windows in and then beat the roof down. They were shouting now over the noise of their hammers and the sound of splintering wood. Their faces had a tense and angry look.

"Hey, cut it out. I'm smashing this bedroom," said Jenny.

"You are not. I got it first," said Elizabeth.

"No, I did," said Harry, and he hit a mighty blow. Jenny shoved him away. "Get away," she said, "it's mine."

"It's mine," said Harry, and slapped her.

"You're a big fat pig," said Jenny, and she kicked him.

"He is not," said Elizabeth. "You are."

Jenny grabbed Elizabeth's hand and pinched it, leaving red fingernail crescents in the skin. Elizabeth scratched Jenny all down her arm. Harry raised his hammer to hit, not the doll house, but his sister. He hit Jenny on her upper arm, and she screamed and kicked him in the stomach, knocking him to the floor.

Babs dashed up the stairs and into her room. "Oh, no!" she screamed. "What have you done? You are monsters! Look at my beautiful doll house. Give me those hammers and get in your rooms at once." She slapped their hands as she grabbed back the hammers.

It was only a few minutes until Babs regained her self-control. She called the children out from their rooms, and told them that she was sorry. "I didn't realize your bad feelings were as strong as this," she said. "There were no children like you in my studies."

All through lunch the children were sulky and cross. Harry spilled his milk, and refused to wipe it up. "I don't care," he said.

"You're a slob, Harry," said Jenny.

"Look who's talking," said Elizabeth.

"I'm going to buy you a big punching bag," said Babs, "and every day you can punch it, and it will help you to calm down."

That afternoon, the children decided to do something really terrible, to see what Babs would do. They didn't enjoy the idea as much as they had at first, but they felt mean and snarly, and it was hard to stop.

"Let's hammer up her picture of 'The Human Child,' " said Harry.

"We can't do anything that bad," said Elizabeth. "It's her favorite thing."

"Well, let's take some of her crazy books about understanding children and make a big bonfire with them," said Jenny.

"Oh, boy," said Harry. "Let's go!"

They stole into Babs's room while she was out buying the punching bag.

"Here's a good one," said Elizabeth, picking up a large blue book, "*A New Look at the Parent-Child Relationship*."

"I've got one," said Jenny. "*A Handbook of Child Psychology*. Why do you suppose they call it a handbook? It weighs a ton."

"What's this one called, Elizabeth?" said Harry. "I can't read it."

"It says *Discipline and Repression*," said Elizabeth. "I don't know what that means."

"Let's take them all," said Jenny.

"We better not," said Elizabeth. "This is plenty."

"You're a sissy," said Jenny.

"I am not," said Elizabeth. "She'll come back before we get the fire going, anyway, if we try to carry them all down."

"Oh, all right," said Jenny.

They carried the books into the backyard and got a supply of kindling from beside the fireplace in the living room. They lit the kindling, and as it blazed up, Harry began an Indian dance around the fire. "Oo-boo-boo-boo-boo," he yelled, hitting his mouth with his hand. Jenny tossed on *A Handbook of Child Psychology.* The fire shot out sparks and sputtered and began to die out.

"It won't burn," she said crossly.

"Take it off, then," said Elizabeth. "We can tear out the pages and throw them on."

Jenny reached in and grabbed it off the fire. "Ow," she yelled. "Look what you made me do, stupid. You made me burn my fingers."

"I did not," said Elizabeth. "You did it yourself, dummy."

The children began to tear out the pages and throw them on the fire, but it was hard slow

work, and they were not having a good time at all. Scowling and silent, they kept it up for pride's sake alone.

It was while they were doing this that Babs returned and found them.

She screamed and began to cry, "Oh, my books, my beautiful books. You are callous, horrible children," she sobbed. "I try. I try so hard. All day long I am working so hard for your sake," and she dashed into the house, leaving the children to watch the fire die down and feel mean.

About an hour later she came down. "I am going back to the Mummy Market," she said. "I can't help you, if you won't let me. It doesn't matter how hard I try. I have arranged for Mrs. O'Flaherty to come and baby-sit for you until Thursday. I only hope for your sakes that you find some genius at the Mummy Market to help you sublimate your terrible hostility. Good-bye. My taxi is waiting."

The children felt too guilty to do anything but stand there and watch her go.

CHAPTER 10

The One in the Empty Booth

Mrs. O'Flaherty arrived soon after Babs had left. She had taken care of the children many times before. She had always come during The Gloom's annual vacation, and the children were fond of her. She cleaned the house and cooked good meals, and let the children alone, except for reminding them to wash their hands before dinner and other small domestic details. Under her solid, calm care the children were able to be more like themselves. By bedtime they were loving each other once again. Elizabeth read aloud *Little House in the Big Woods* to Harry and Jenny, and they went to bed feeling as if they had got over some sickness, rather like getting well after the measles.

In the morning, of course, the first thing they did was to go and see Mrs. Cavour. Her garden was at its most beautiful now. Great spires of delphiniums—blue, white, and lavender—seemed to hang in the air over the other plants. The first of the annuals—zinnias, snapdragons, salvia, petunias, marigolds, verbena, and marguerites— were making bright spots of color through the white clouds of shasta daisies, feverfew, baby's breath, and early white phlox. The tomato vines were taller than the dark peony bushes now, and the first tassels were showing on the corn.

Mrs. Cavour was gathering rose petals when they found her.

"What are you doing that for?" asked Jenny.

"To make potpourri, so I can smell the roses all winter," she said. "I'll give you some when it's finished, if you like."

"Oh, yes. Thank you," said Jenny.

"Did you find the right mother?" said Mrs. Cavour.

"No. We don't get any better at choosing them," said Elizabeth.

"This one was sort of so-so, but she made us be all funny," said Harry.

"We were the ones that were horrible with her," said Elizabeth.

"How did that happen?" said Mrs. Cavour.

The children were unable to explain quite why they had been so mean to poor Babs, but when they told Mrs. Cavour the whole story, she seemed to understand, anyway.

"We picked the one who said she understood children," said Elizabeth, "and it turned out just as bad as the others."

"I hate them all," said Jenny. "I wish we could find our own mother."

"My dear," said Mrs. Cavour. "What did you expect to find at the Mummy Market? Surely not someone else's mother?"

All the children began shouting at once, and for a little while Mrs. Cavour could make nothing of what they said. Finally, Jenny's voice could be distinguished, because she was angry and it was very loud.

"Why didn't you tell us?" she shouted. "You mean our own mother is there and you never told us? Boy, I don't think that's fair."

"We would never have picked Babs if we knew that," said Elizabeth. "She couldn't be anyone's mother."

"For sure not ours, anyway," said Harry.

"We certainly have misunderstood each other," said Mrs. Cavour as she shook the petals off a low pink rose called Souvenir de la Malmaison. "I thought it was quite clear that you were looking for your mother."

"We didn't think we had one," said Elizabeth.

"That's a typical manifestation of the enchantment," said Mrs. Cavour, moving on to a yellow rose called Rêve d'Or.

"The WHAT?" said Jenny, or rather, shouted Jenny.

"Enchantment. Sorcery. Its name doesn't matter. It is what has taken away your mother."

"I don't understand," said Elizabeth, who was nearly crying. "If we have one, why don't we remember her?"

"Naturally you don't remember her. Memory would break the spell. That is the way of enchantment," said Mrs. Cavour. "When you do break it and get her back, you will remember quite clearly. She isn't lost, you know. Only mislaid."

"Are you sure you're not teasing us?" said Elizabeth.

"Quite," said Mrs. Cavour.

"How can we find her?" said Harry.

"Who enchanted her, anyway?" said Jenny.

"That needn't concern you," said Mrs. Cavour. "The sources of enchantment are many and difficult."

"What do you mean, *not* concern us?" said Jenny. "She's our mother, isn't she?"

"I mean that the story isn't about how the prince became a frog, but about how the princess turned him back into a prince. As a matter of fact, some degree of enchantment is so nearly universal nowadays that it ceases to be of any real interest."

"I don't think it's so universal," said Elizabeth. "I don't know anyone who got turned into something. You're mixing me up."

"Frogs and beasts have gone out of style," said Mrs. Cavour. She scooped up a handful of rose petals, and let them fall like multicolored rain back into the basket. She sighed, and Elizabeth thought that perhaps she was remembering with regret the days before frogs and beasts had gone out of style.

"The Gloom is a good example of a contemporary enchantment," said Mrs. Cavour. "What is she? A person or a housekeeper?"

"A housekeeper," said Elizabeth.

"Perhaps a more horrid fate than being a frog," said Mrs. Cavour.

"Who cares about The Gloom?" said Jenny rudely. "How do we get our mother?"

"The method hasn't changed since the days of frogs and princes," said Mrs. Cavour. "You must choose her."

"But how do we recognize her?" said Elizabeth.

"Now that you know who you are looking for, it should be easier," said Mrs. Cavour.

"Will you make us some flower magic the way you did before, so we'll know her?" said Harry.

"You'll have to make your own," said Mrs. Cavour. "After all, she's your own mother."

"How do we do that? We don't know any magic," said Elizabeth.

"A spell isn't essential, you know," said Mrs. Cavour. "But a nice one can't hurt. You might see what happens if you say the names of wild flowers."

"I can't think of any," said Jenny.

"Just think of the places they grow," said

Mrs. Cavour. "Think of the woods, and swamps in spring, and fields in summer."

"Daisies," said Harry.

"Good," said Mrs. Cavour.

"Goldenrod," said Jenny.

"Violets, buttercups . . . oh, I know, lady slippers—pink ones and yellow ones," said Elizabeth very fast.

"Daisies," said Harry.

"You already said that," said Jenny.

"I like daisies," said Harry. "I want them in again."

"Devil's paintbrush and skunk cabbage," said Jenny.

"Take it back," said Elizabeth.

"Your mother isn't perfect, you know," said Mrs. Cavour. "Skunk cabbage is the first flower to bloom in the spring. I for one am always very glad to see it."

"Black-eyed Susans," said Harry.

"Good for you, Harry," said Elizabeth.

"Spiderwort," said Jenny.

"You made that up," said Elizabeth. "You're making it be all dreadful."

"I did not," said Jenny. "It's real. Mrs. Cavour even showed it to me. It's blue. I'm only trying to make it sound more like a spell."

"It's a beautiful flower, too," said Mrs. Cavour. "Don't worry about names. There is even a quite nice one called viper's bugloss."

"Daisies," said Harry.

"Wild roses and water lilies," said Elizabeth.

"Forget-me-nots," said Jenny proudly.

"That ought to be adequate," said Mrs. Cavour. "And it certainly sounds like you. I am sure it will be a help to you at the Mummy Market."

"Maybe we should try that one with the empty booth," said Elizabeth.

"Is there one in an empty booth?" said Mrs. Cavour. "She sounds well worth talking to. Don't get discouraged, and remember '*Ad matrem per aspera.*'"

"What does that mean?" said Elizabeth.

"It means 'It is hard work to find out who your mother is,'" said Mrs. Cavour.

The next morning, when Jenny woke up, she felt cross and unhappy. She didn't even want to go to the Mummy Market. Elizabeth wondered if it was because of the skunk cabbage and spiderworts in the spell, but she didn't say so.

"I don't believe our own mother is there,"

said Jenny to Elizabeth. "I think they're all the same. You think you've picked the right one and you feel all nice for a while, and then they turn out horrible. I'm sick of them. I'd rather keep Mrs. O'Flaherty."

"Mrs. Cavour said to try that one with the empty booth," said Elizabeth. "You're being like me when I didn't believe her about going to the Mummy Market the first time."

"I am not," said Jenny, more crossly than truthfully. "I believe Mrs. Cavour. It's just those mothers. They all find a new way to be icky that you would never have thought of."

"Oh, come on, Jenny," said Harry. "I want our real mother, not just a sort-of-all-right lady like Mrs. O'Flaherty."

"She's going home after lunch, anyway. Babs only hired her till then," said Elizabeth. "If you believe Mrs. Cavour, like you said, you'd go and talk to that empty-booth one. Besides, if you really believe Mrs. Cavour, think of our own mother caught in that enchantment and us not rescuing her."

"Do you believe that?" asked Jenny.

"I don't know," said Elizabeth. "Maybe not

all of it. But it was true about the Mummy Market, wasn't it?"

"It is so true," said Harry. "Mrs. Cavour wouldn't tell it to us if it wasn't true."

Gradually, Elizabeth and Harry convinced Jenny that she should give the mother with only a chair in her stall a try. She agreed to come, partly to please Elizabeth and Harry, and partly because she was not the kind of person who could abandon her mother in an enchantment without first trying every possible way to free her. But her heart was not really in it, and her fear of their choosing yet another terrible mother did not leave her.

On the way to the Mummy Market, Harry was worried that the mother might have been taken. Elizabeth assured him that if she were really their own mother, she would be there waiting for them; but in her heart of hearts she was feeling the same worry. When they arrived at the market, Elizabeth and Harry ran straight toward her booth, and felt lifted up with relief when they saw she was still there. They waited for Jenny to catch up, and then walked slowly up to her.

She smiled at them, but didn't say anything. Elizabeth smiled back. Jenny scowled.

"How come you don't have anything in your booth?" she said.

"I do have something. I have myself in it," said the mother.

"What are you like?" said Harry.

"That's sort of hard to answer," said the mother. "Do you want me to tell you how old I am and how tall I am and that kind of thing?"

"No," said Harry. He thought a while. "Can you cook?" he said.

"Yes," said the mother. "I'm a good cook, but I'm a bit messy. I hate picking up. What are you like?"

"I don't know," said Harry. "I'm just me."

"Well, what kind of things do you like?" said the mother.

"I like machines and fish and birds and worms and pollywogs and snakes. I like things like that," said Harry.

"Do you like it when you find a good piece of chain or a bird's nest?" said the mother.

"Yes," said Harry. "How did you know?"

"I get that way myself sometimes," said the

mother. She turned to Elizabeth. "What sort of things do you like?" she said.

"I like books," said Elizabeth. "I mean some of them. I don't like the kind that gives you the feeling they're trying to improve your mind. I like the kind that tells you things you almost already knew. I think I like horses and babies. I wish I had a garden like this lady we know named Mrs. Cavour."

"Do you?" said the mother. "I love gardens, too. And woods and things like that. What about you?" she said to Jenny.

"I don't know," said Jenny, shrugging her shoulders.

"Oh," said the mother. She shifted her position in her chair as if she felt uncomfortable.

"Have you had a lot of different children before?" asked Harry.

"No. I just keep feeling that I need to be someone's mother."

"Didn't you get traded in?" asked Elizabeth.

"No. I heard about the Mummy Market, and I asked the Selection Committee if I could come, and they said Yes. But I'm getting a bit discouraged. No one has picked me."

Harry didn't even wait until they could discuss her privately.

"We want you," he said.

Elizabeth nodded. "Yes," she said. "We really do."

Jenny didn't say anything.

"Oh, I'm terribly pleased," said the mother. "Do you think I'll be all right?"

"Yes," said Elizabeth. "You can learn. We'll teach you."

"Shall I come right now?" said the mother.

"Yes," said Harry. "Right away. We need you."

"Good," said the mother. "I certainly need you, too." She picked up a small suitcase from the back of her stall and jumped down with the children.

CHAPTER 11

Yesterday

On the way home, everyone but Jenny was conscious of a little shyness in the air around them. On the bus, they didn't talk much. Elizabeth looked at the mother and smiled and then looked quickly out the window as if she hadn't meant to be looking in that direction at all. Harry kept twisting his feet together and staring at them. Jenny sat heavily and moved very little.

"Is it all right with you if you call me Mummy?" said their new mother. "When I was sitting in that booth I kept imagining being called that."

"Yes," said Harry.

Conversations would start like that, and then simply stop all by themselves.

When they got home, they showed Mummy to her room. She put down her suitcase and looked around the room, and an expression that was a little sad and empty came on her face.

"Will you show me *your* rooms, please?" she said, sounding formal and distant.

First, they took her to Harry's room. "What a lovely iguana," she said. "You must be very proud of him."

"I am," said Harry.

She admired Elizabeth's room, and looked carefully at the books in the bookshelf.

In Jenny's room, she patted the teddy bear who was lying on the bed.

"Please don't do that," said Jenny politely but coldly. "He doesn't like strangers to pat him."

"I'm terribly sorry," said Mummy, pulling her hand back and standing very still. "Maybe I should go down and see about fixing dinner."

Jenny felt anger and loneliness rise up in her. She stood still, looking at the door where Mummy had gone out.

"What's the matter with you?" said Elizabeth in a fierce whisper. "Why do you keep being so mean to her?"

"I don't keep being mean to her," said Jenny. "You and Harry were mean to pick her without talking about it first. You just said you wanted her and didn't even ask me what I thought."

"Don't you like her?" said Elizabeth.

"Maybe she's okay, and maybe she isn't," said Jenny. "I'm just not going to trust her until I find out for sure. That's what we did with those others. We thought they were fine, and then they turned out to be terrible."

"You'll make her go back to the Mummy Market if you keep being mean to her," said Harry.

"If she quits, she's not our mother at all," said Jenny. "She's just a housekeeper. People's mothers don't quit."

Harry began to cry.

"Don't you be mean to Mummy," he shouted. "I'll punch you and hit you and kick you if you're mean."

"Don't cry, Harry. Jenny's right. If she's ours, she won't quit," said Elizabeth, putting her arms around him. "Wait a second and let me think. I've almost got something figured out."

"What?" said Harry, sniffing.

"Well, suppose maybe—if Mrs. Cavour is telling the truth—suppose Mimsy and Mom and Babs were all enchantments, and Mummy is real."

"Here's a Kleenex, Harry," said Jenny kindly.

"Do you mean our real mummy?" said Harry.

"I don't know," said Elizabeth. "But she makes us all feel different than the others did. She feels solider. Jenny gets really mean to her; you get really sad about it. We all feel shy. Why didn't we feel shy with Mom and Babs and Mimsey? I think it's because they weren't real, and Mummy is."

"How come we don't remember her, then?" said Jenny.

"I don't think just picking her at the Mummy Market is enough to break the enchantment. If there is one," said Elizabeth. "I think we have to choose her, really and truly. Each one of us. It can't break the enchantment if Jenny still hasn't chosen her."

"I see what you mean, I think," said Jenny,

who felt a lot nicer when she could think that it was perhaps the fault of the enchantment that she had been so mean to Mummy. "Like the princess had to shut her eyes and put her arms around the frog."

"Yes," said Elizabeth. "Just marrying him didn't do the trick."

"I don't know if I choose her really and truly yet," said Jenny. "But I'll go down and tell her I'm sorry, and set the table. She doesn't know where anything is."

Jenny ran down the stairs and found that Mummy really was in need of help in the kitchen. The others came in and sat on the counter by the refrigerator, but Jenny was the one who showed Mummy where everything was. Maybe because she needed their help, they did not feel so shy of her anymore, and they told her all about the Mummy Market and their unsuccessful mothers, and about Mrs. Cavour and her garden. But they didn't tell her about the enchantment, and their hopes for rescuing her from it. Somehow they felt it would be quite rude to mention the enchantment (if there was one) while she was still in its grip.

Talking to Mummy was delightful. She listened with a deep and happy seriousness to everything they said. They went right on talking all through dinner, leaving the Mummy Market far behind, and telling her about many sides of their lives.

"I wish we had lots of memories together," said Mummy when dinner was finished. "I feel all empty for them, I miss them so much. Let's leave the dishes and go outside and talk some more."

They went out the back door into the yard. Mummy sat down comfortably and pulled up a white clover leaf and began to chew on its stem. The children lay flat on the grass. Jenny poked at the blades, separating them and watching little ants creeping away. Elizabeth and Harry lay on their backs and looked at the sky and the birds hurrying to catch a few more bugs before dark.

Elizabeth poked Jenny meaningfully with her elbow. "We know just how you feel about the memories," she said encouragingly to Mummy.

"Do you think we could make some?" said Mummy.

"You mean, do things together so we can remember them?" asked Jenny.

"Well, yes, but I mean make ones about our

past, when you were babies and all," said Mummy. "I feel as if I practically could remember it all, as if it were just around some corner in my mind."

"How do you make a memory?" said Harry.

"Do you suppose we could think very carefully about how it was, and then tell each other?" said Mummy.

"I don't know," said Elizabeth. "Why don't you try? Make one about me. Make one when I was a baby."

Mummy looked at her carefully and smiled.

"Well, maybe once," she said, "when you were new, it was a little like it is now—I mean we hadn't known each other very long. And you know what I think maybe I did? I used to be shy to kiss you as much as I wanted, because you were so tiny and I wanted to kiss you almost all day long. So I would hold you and look at you and say, 'Well, I will just kiss her once, on the top of her head,' and then I would get carried away and kiss you all the way down to your toes. I think maybe it was like that."

Elizabeth laughed and pulled her knees up under her chin and hugged herself.

"Do you really think it was that way?" she

said. "Did you always get carried away?"

"Yes," said Mummy. "Always."

"Make one about me," said Harry. "But not when I'm a baby. Make one when I'm grown up."

"You'll have to help me, then," said Mummy. "I can't do that kind alone. What do you do when you're grown up?"

"I'm a crane man," said Harry. "I run a giant crane."

"Is it a yellow one?" said Mummy.

"No. It's green," said Harry.

Mummy chewed on a new piece of clover.

"Well," she said, "you are a big crane man, and you have a huge green crane; and some-times you lift great steel beams with it to build great buildings, and sometimes you have a round steel ball hanging on the end and you swing it against old buildings and you smash them all down."

"It isn't a round ball," said Harry. "It's shaped like a drop."

"Thank you," said Mummy. "I didn't know that. Well, after you have smashed buildings and built buildings all day long, you put your crane away and you go home." She paused and Harry sighed happily.

"Are you married?" said Mummy.

"Yes," said Harry.

"Well, your wife is terribly glad to see you when you get home, because she missed you all day. And your children . . . how many children do you have, Harry?"

"I have five," said Harry firmly. "All boys. No girls."

"Your children can hardly wait for you to get home, because tomorrow is Saturday and you promised you would take them fishing."

"Yes," said Harry. "Go on."

"That's all for now," said Mummy. "It isn't a good idea to tell too much of someone else's memories that didn't happen yet."

Harry smiled. "You know why we have to come home after we went fishing?" he said.

"No. Why?" said Mummy.

"Because our grandmother is coming to spend the night."

"Is that me?" said Mummy.

"Yes."

"Oh, Harry," said Mummy.

"Make one for me," said Jenny. "An exciting one. Make an adventure, one that happened yesterday to all of us."

"Yesterday is hard," said Mummy. "We remember it so clearly. And we all have to make it if we were all there. Where were we, anyway?"

"We went on a picnic," said Harry.

"In the woods, where we had never been before," said Jenny. "We followed a brook to find out where it started."

"No, we didn't," said Harry. "We went to Fox Hill Pond, and I caught a fish."

"*I* didn't," said Elizabeth. "I went to the beach. The real beach by the ocean."

"You know what we did?" said Mummy. "The reason it was such an adventure is that we couldn't decide which one to do, so we did them all."

"We did?" said Jenny, sitting straight up.

"Yes," said Mummy. "We slept very late this morning, we were so tired. But it was heavenly."

"What happened?" said Jenny.

"We had decided it the night before," said Mummy. "And we got up when it was still dark and—oh, dear, do we have a car, Jenny?"

"Yes," said Jenny. "There's one in the garage. The Gloom had it to take us to the dentist."

"We got to the beach before the sun came up," said Mummy. "And there was no one there but us. It was like being on the edge of the land and the edge of the sea and the edge of the day all at once. The color of the fire we made of driftwood and the color of the sunrise were almost the same. You tell about it, Elizabeth. You were the one who picked the beach."

While the sun went down, in their own backyard they laughed and shouted and interrupted one another and crowded everything they could possibly fit into a perfectly glorious yesterday. They had cooked breakfast over the driftwood fire, and then they had climbed to the top of the round dunes (the dry sand was just warming in the sun), and had run leaping and sliding down to play with the waves. When the day grew older, and more people began to come, they had left the beach and had followed Jenny's brook. It was a little brook, and its clear brown pools were not even knee deep, but still it had swamps and tangled brush to wade through. Their arms and legs were scratched and they were hot and their sneakers made wet, squashy noises when they walked, but they had found where it began in a spring bubbling up from between moss-covered rocks. Mummy said that all around was a bank of thick, deep star moss, and they had all lain down and slept, since they had woken up so early. Jenny doubted that she herself had slept at all.

Harry had caught his fish in the evening, when the water of the pond was perfectly still and pale and the trees around were dark. The swallows had swooped so low, chasing insects, that their wings had ruffled the water, and the insects had flown so close to the still surface that sometimes they bumped against it, and little dimpled places came and went in the shining water. Harry told of the splash and the tug on his line. Jenny said that the fish was a sucker and they had to throw it back; but Harry didn't mind, because that meant it was still alive, and Elizabeth said it was the biggest sucker they had ever seen, and Mummy said it looked as if it were made all of silver.

Gradually, they stopped talking and lay silent on the grass, thinking about their memories. And after a while, when the stars began to come out in the pale sky, and the dew made the grass against their skin feel damp and cold, they got up and went into the house.

CHAPTER 12

The Garden

The final dissolving of the enchantment took place while they slept. This was fortunate, because although rescuing one's mother from enchantment is rewarding work, it is exhausting. All night long, as naturally as the stars came out in the sky, their own true memories came out in their minds; and while new stars rose in the east and old ones set in the west, their memories rose up in their dreams, sorted themselves, and settled down where they belonged. As Mrs. Cavour had said, the same effect as having The Gloom go up in a puff of smoke was achieved nowadays by more subtle means.

When the children woke up in the morning, their memories had settled so accurately that they did not even feel surprise. Of course they had recovered their mother and with her all the true yesterdays. Last night was true, and the yesterday they had told to each other was true. It cannot be said for sure that it all took place in one day—the sea and the brook and the pond— because when an enchantment breaks, it is sometimes like a dam breaking and the truth may rush in at first like a flood. Nor could they be sure of the exact point when they had lost their mother and she had been replaced by The Gloom. It is in the nature of enchantment that it is nearly impossible to detect its encroachment, even as it closes round its victim.

Elizabeth lay in bed listening to the song sparrows, and she thought she knew what was making them so happy. Then she heard Jenny's recorder, which had not been played since Jenny had been a bugler, and it sounded as joyful as the birds. Harry came in and bounced on her bed. "Wake up, wake up," he said. "Breakfast is ready."

Breakfast took a very long time. They could hardly stop talking about all the things they wanted to do. Elizabeth was going to make a garden in the backyard. Mummy was going to learn how to play an alto recorder and play duets with Jenny. Harry was going to build a birchbark canoe, and they would all float down rivers and paddle silently across wide lakes.

"Let's start the garden today," said Elizabeth. "It's not too late, is it?"

"There are lots of things you can plant now," said Mummy. "Radishes and lettuce and bachelor's buttons and nasturtiums and zinnias."

"Mrs. Cavour said that good mothers are rather like zinnias," said Jenny. "She said they were a bit ordinary but very dependable."

"She did?" said Mummy. "They aren't ordinary at all. They may be dependable, but they're not one bit ordinary. Plant lots of zinnias, Elizabeth."

"Oh, Mummy," said Elizabeth. "Don't be silly. We don't think you're ordinary."

"Let's start right now," said Harry.

"You know what I'm going to do?" said Mummy, jumping to her feet. "I know a place where they might still have seedlings for sale, maybe even zinnias. I'll get some seeds, too. You pick a place for the garden and start digging, and I'll be back as fast as I can."

They all went out to the backyard, and the children were pleased, but not surprised, when Mummy went straight to the garage and drove off in the car—the one The Gloom had used for trips to the dentist. Elizabeth found the shovel, and dragged it behind her while they walked around the yard to choose their garden plot. They picked a sunny place against the fence, where their plants wouldn't be broken by kickball games and other local hazards. They took turns digging, turning over big chunks of earth, and the two who weren't digging squatted down and broke up the chunks with their hands.

They heard the car drive up, and ran to meet Mummy. She stepped out with her face shining. "Look," she said, "success," and held up a flat wooden box full of small green plants. She fished a paper bag out of the car and turned it upside down. Out fell packets of seeds with the most tantalizing pictures of perfect red radishes, huge orange and yellow nasturtiums, ruffled lettuce, and string beans without a blemish. "They had just one flat of zinnias left," she said. "But they said they could get us some petunias and tomatoes tomorrow. Next year, we'll start earlier and grow them all from seed."

The children gathered up the seed packets

and led Mummy to their garden. "That's wonderful," said Mummy. "We can plant the zinnias right away. Can you get the hose, Elizabeth?"

"I will," said Harry. He ran off and returned dragging the hose with water gushing from it. Mummy showed them how to scoop a little hole in the prepared ground, fill it with water, and set one of the plants in it. She separated the roots of the zinnias; Jenny scooped out the holes, Harry filled them with water, and Elizabeth put the little seedlings into the mud and pushed the loose dirt in around them. When the last one was planted and the dirt firmly patted down, they stood back to admire their garden. Their faces had black smudges on them and their hands were all mud up beyond their wrists. Elizabeth sighed with pleasure. Harry took the shovel and dug out a big scoop, filled it with water from the hose, and stepped into the pool and squished the mud between his toes.

"Do you want me to plant you, Harry?" said Elizabeth.

Harry smiled. "Watch," he said. "I can make rainbows." He put his thumb over the end of the hose, and sprayed the water straight up in the air toward the top of the sky, higher than

the sun had yet climbed. Jenny and Elizabeth
and Mummy jumped back as the water came
sprinkling down on them. Harry laughed and
let it fall all over him and the garden. The drops
were sparkling and shimmering in the blue air,
and hung arching through them was the rain-
bow.

"Oh, Mummy, Mummy, Mummy, I'm so
glad you're here," said Jenny.

Harry lowered the hose and Elizabeth stuck
her hands in the water, and wiped them on the
grass. She looked up at Jenny. "Can we ask
Mummy up to the tree house?" she said.

"Yes. Do come, Mummy," said Jenny.

"It has a password," said Harry. "It's—"

"Shh," said Mummy, putting her hands over her ears. "Don't tell me your password. If I knew it, I could just come. I'd rather be invited."

The children climbed the ladder like monkeys, but when Mummy tried, her feet pushed away the bottom of the ladder, and she was left dangling. The children watched her with concern.

"You have to pull harder with your hands," said Elizabeth.

"And sort of pull back with your feet so they stay under you," said Jenny.

This time Mummy reached the platform. She sat down on the floor and leaned against the wall.

"Thank you," she said. "This is the best invitation I ever had."

Elizabeth pulled up the ladder and bunched it up on the very edge of the platform, it was so crowded in the tree house. They sat with their knees drawn up and their feet all tangled together in the middle of the floor. They could hear the cars and the trucks on the streets, sounding unreal and far away. The breeze was just enough to move the little flecks of sunshine that filtered through the leaves, speckling all four of them with gold. The leaves barely rustled, and when a mosquito came whining by, he sounded absurdly loud. Harry waved him away. Jenny moved over a few inches and leaned against Mummy. Mummy smiled and put her arm around her. Elizabeth crossed her arms on her knees and rested her head on them. It seemed to her as if the tree house was hung halfway between earth and sky, warm and secret and only for them.

Mummy smoothed the hair out of Jenny's eyes.

"Where were you when The Gloom was here?" said Harry.

"I could never have been very far from you," said Mummy. "I'm even gladder than you are that I'm here."

"We'll never trade you in," said Harry.

"I don't think we could even find the Mummy Market now," said Mummy. "I think it was just the weak spot in the enchantment. The crack in the wall."

Elizabeth lifted her head in alarm. "What about Mrs. Cavour?" she said. "What about her garden? That's there, isn't it?"

"That's always there," said Mummy. "I don't think any enchantment can touch it."

"But she has spells and flower magic," said Elizabeth. "Isn't that the same?"

"No. She does that for the fun of it. Everything in her garden is real. Even the rose bugs. Try to image Babs in there talking to Mrs. Cavour. There isn't any room for enchantment in there."

"I don't think it can get in our tree house," said Jenny, looking around her.

"No. Thank goodness for that," said Mummy. "The Gloom and Mimsey and Mom and all couldn't come here any more than to Mrs. Cavour's. I'll tell you a flower poem, like Mrs. Cavour's, or at least a bit of one. It's the end of a lullaby, and I think it tells about the places where enchantment can't enter—where it has to stop: 'Leaving you alone with what is yours, like a garden with a mass of melissas and star anise.'"

Elizabeth was silent, wondering what a garden of melissas and star anise was like, but Harry and Jenny spoke at the same time. "What are melissas and star anise?" they said.

"Mrs. Cavour can tell you," said Mummy. "Why don't you go and ask her?"

CHAPTER 13

A Midsummer's Day

The children wheeled their bicycles through Mrs. Cavour's singing hedge late in the morning. The day was turning out to be one of those days that come once in a while in July, when the clearness of the air is almost frightening because it is a reminder that summer will not last forever.

They found Mrs. Cavour scowling and muttering at the Japanese beetles on her roses.

"Are you putting a spell on them?" asked Harry.

"Oh, no," she said. "I couldn't do that. It would be like spraying them. There is no joy in an unequal battle. Are you pleased with your mother?"

"Oh, yes," said Elizabeth.

"We planted a garden," said Harry.

"What are melissas and star anise?" said Jenny.

"Did your mother tell you that? You certainly have broken the enchantment," said Mrs. Cavour, picking off a Japanese beetle.

"Well, what are they?" said Harry.

"I'll let you find out," said Mrs. Cavour. "We'll play a game. Do you know how to play 'Hot or Cold'? That's the game that when you get close to what you're looking for, someone tells you you're getting warmer. We'll play it with the weather. I'll tell you you're in summer when you're close or in winter when you're far, and you hunt for them. Where you are now is like a warm day in November when you remember summer, but there are no leaves on the trees."

The children, followed by Mrs. Cavour, moved off from the tangle of roses to where the feathery corn tassels were standing among the hollyhocks.

"Bad killing frost," said Mrs. Cavour.

They ran across the shade-patterned grass to the trunks of the enormous sugar maples.

"Worse yet. Ice storm. Severe damage to trees," said Mrs. Cavour.

They followed along the hedge to where brilliant red and orange turk's cap lilies were poking through the dead blossoms of a smoke bush.

"January thaw. Hint of spring," said Mrs. Cavour.

They doubled across the front of the house to where the bees were humming at the veronicas and petunias.

"Blizzard. Gale winds and subzero temperatures," said Mrs. Cavour. "Here, pull yourselves some carrots. You can sometimes think better if you are crunching one."

They wiped the dirt off on their shorts, and turned the corner of the house under the grape arbor.

"Spring day. First crocus," said Mrs. Cavour.

They followed the other wall of the vine-covered house.

"Late frost. Lost some tomato seedlings," said Mrs. Cavour.

Jenny jumped over a low hedge of sweetfern into an herb garden with the plants twisting in and out of each other in a knotted pattern.

"Baltimore orioles arrive in town," said Mrs. Cavour.

On the other side of the herb garden was a thick grove of small hemlocks, with a stone wall behind them and stone steps showing a narrow passage between the touching hemlock branches. Harry bounded over to them.

"A midsummer's day," said Mrs. Cavour.

The children ran up the steps and found themselves in a small, triangular hidden garden. They had never known it was there. It was surrounded on two sides by the hedge, and on the other by the stone wall and the grove of hemlocks. The air in it was still except for the bees and the softer sound of a startled hummingbird. The ground was carpeted with a low, creeping mintlike plant, and standing in the center were three small trees, like magnolias, with long leaves and a small green star-shaped fruit.

"The trees are star anise," said Mrs. Cavour, "and the little white flowers the bees love so are melissas. It's common garden balm. The Greeks named it for the bees, and a friend of my family's, a Mr. Hunter, said, 'It driveth away all poisons arising from melancholy.' "

"Why does it smell so sweet?" said Jenny.

"That's what it is: sweet balm," said Mrs. Cavour.

"Can we take some home to Mummy?" said Harry.

"Yes," said Mrs. Cavour. "Pick all the sweet balm you can carry, and I will break you some branches of star anise."

The children started filling their hands and arms, and as they broke the stems the sweet mint and anise fragrance filled the small walled garden and the warm air that hung over it.

Mrs. Cavour walked with them back to their

bicycles. They filled their baskets with the flowers. Elizabeth fitted hers in neatly, stems down, but Jenny's and Harry's were every which way.

"Thank you, Mrs. Cavour," said Elizabeth, "for the flowers and for the Mummy Market."

"Well, my dear," said Mrs. Cavour, watching Harry shoving his flowers into his basket. "Just because you don't do things in the order that other children do them in doesn't mean that you won't do them at all."

"Good-bye, Mrs. Cavour. Good-bye, good-bye," said the children, and they wheeled their flower-laden bicycles carefully out of the garden.

When they reached the road, Harry shouted, "Yippee," and jumped in the air kicking his heels together before he mounted his bike. They all rode off, weaving back and forth across the road because they were so happy.

Melissa and star anise fragrance surrounded them, and petals and whole flowers fell from their baskets into the road.